To George,

Thank u for the most
memorable years of my life.

Love
Diana '83

Brooke Meanley

Waterfowl

of the Chesapeake Bay Country

By Brooke Meanley

WATERFOWL
OF THE
CHESAPEAKE BAY
COUNTRY

BY BROOKE MEANLEY
WITH DRAWINGS BY JOHN W. TAYLOR

TIDEWATER PUBLISHERS
CENTREVILLE, MARYLAND

Library of Congress Cataloging in Publication Data

Meanley, Brooke.
    Waterfowl of the Chesapeake Bay country.

    Bibliography: p.
    Includes index.
    1. Waterfowl—Chesapeake Bay (Md. and Va.)
2. Birds—Chesapeake Bay (Md. and Va.) I. Title.
QL696.A5M387   598.4'109755'18   81-18361
ISBN 0-87033-281-3   AACR2

Manufactured in the United States of America
First edition

Contents

v

Waterfowl of the Chesapeake Bay Country

Foreword

This volume is intended to be a general account of waterfowl of the Chesapeake Bay country, with emphasis on their distribution, abundance, and ecology. There have been numerous technical reports and papers on this subject published by various scientific institutions. Most have been concerned with the Maryland section of the Bay and are not generally known or readily available to the layman.

The best known such study is that of Robert E. Stewart of the U.S. Fish and Wildlife Service whose report, entitled *Waterfowl Populations in the Upper Chesapeake Region*, appeared in 1962. Stewart's report has served as a guide and important source of information for this book. Other sources were *Birds of Maryland and the District of Columbia* (1958) by Robert E. Stewart and C.S. Robbins; *Maryland Birdlife*, publication of the Maryland Ornithological Society; the Christmas Bird Counts that appear in *American Birds*, published by the National Audubon Society; *Summary of Available Information on Chesapeake Bay Submerged Vegetation* (1978) by J. Court

Figure 1. A Canada goose drinking. The "honker" is the most abundant waterfowl species wintering in Chesapeake Bay. Photograph: Rex Gary Schmidt, USFWS.

Figure 2. Whistling swans. Birds with duller head and neck plumage are immatures. About forty-five thousand wintered on Chesapeake Bay in 1979. Photograph: Luther Goldman.

Figure 3. Most canvasbacks occur in the shallower parts of large embayments and about halfway between the beginning of the tidal section of a river and its mouth, e.g., the Potomac off King George and Westmoreland counties, Virginia; the Patuxent near Benedict; the Nanticoke opposite Bivalve; and the Rappahannock below Tappahannock. Photograph: G. Michael Haramis, USFWS.

Stevenson and Nedra M. Confer of the University of Maryland Horn Point Environmental Laboratories; *Handbook of North American Birds* (Waterfowl, parts 1 & 2) (1976) edited by Ralph S. Palmer; *Ducks, Geese and Swans of North America* (1976) by Frank Bellrose; and census reports of the Office of Migratory Bird Management, U.S. Fish and Wildlife Service.

Waterfowl research in Chesapeake Bay has been continuous since the 1930s. Francis M. Uhler, biologist with the U.S. Fish and Wildlife Service for fifty years, is still continuing his work on waterfowl food habits. Vernon D. Stotts of the Maryland Wildlife Administration has been monitoring waterfowl populations in the Bay since the 1950s; his specialty is the black duck. Current research of whistling swans (Figure 2) is under the direction of William J.L. Sladen of Johns Hopkins University; and studies of the canvasback (Figure 3), begun in the early 1970s by the Fish and Wildlife Service, are being continued by Matthew C. Perry and G. Michael Haramis.

My interest in Chesapeake Bay waterfowl began in the late 1920s, with field trips to Grace's Quarter, Carroll's Island, and the Gunpowder and Bird rivers. Prior to that time my earliest recollection of wild ducks was as a young boy living in Baltimore County, Maryland, when my next door neighbor, John Hayward, brought back a brace of canvasbacks from a hunting trip and hung them on a shutter outside of his window for a few days to "ripen" a little bit so they would be *gamier* when placed on the table!

In the writing of this book, I have had help from many quarters. I am indebted to my colleagues in the U.S. Fish and Wildlife Service for their many favors, especially Matthew C. Perry, G. Michael Haramis, Francis M. Uhler, Luther C. Goldman, Robert E. Stewart, Morton M. Smith, Warren Blandin, James R. Goldsberry, and Danny Bystrak. Others who have helped with advice and material are Samuel A. Grimes, wildlife photographer; John W. Taylor, Chesapeake Bay waterfowl artist, and Gorman M. Bond, ornithologist. I thank them all, and my wife Anna, who edited the manuscript.

xi

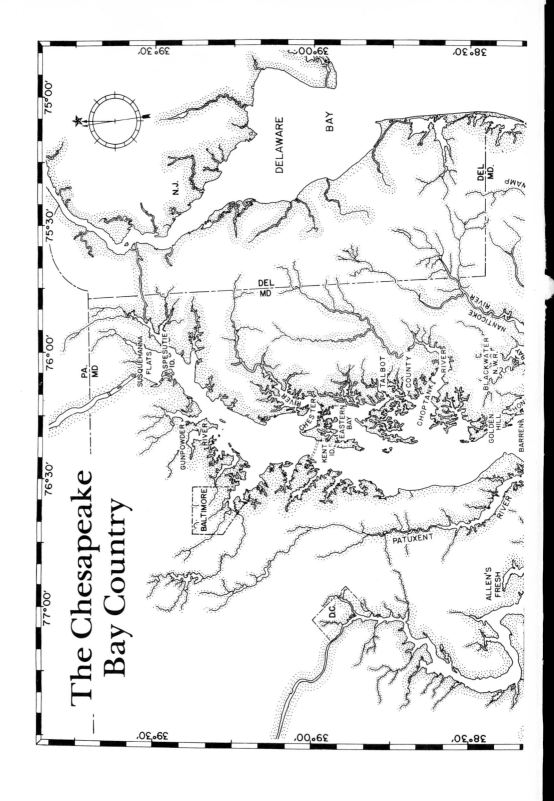

The Chesapeake
Bay Country

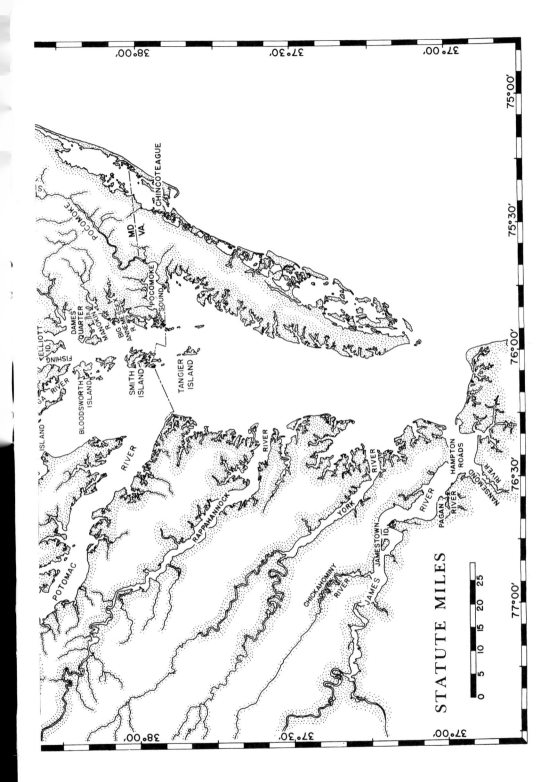

STATUTE MILES

0   5   10   15   20   25

Waterfowl

of the Chesapeake Bay Country

1

Chesapeake Bay— a Good Place for Waterfowl

Every fall an estimated million waterfowl migrate from northern breeding grounds to the Chesapeake Bay to spend the winter. The Bay is also the focal point for another million that stop over enroute to wintering grounds along the South Atlantic Coastal Plain. Some of the waterfowl come from as far away as the Bering Sea Coast of Alaska and the Arctic coast of northern Greenland. Most come from southern Canada and some from our northern tier of states.

The present size of the wintering population is about twenty percent less than it was twenty-five years ago, and the structure has changed. There has been a marked increase in the Canada goose population (Figure 4), and a decline in the number of dabbling ducks and divers. The number of waterfowl wintering in Chesapeake Bay is about twenty-five percent of the waterfowl using the Atlantic flyway.

Chesapeake Bay, in the heart of the Atlantic Flyway, is a prime wintering area for waterfowl because of its size, location, diversity

Figure 4. Canada geese on a frozen pond, lower Kent County, Maryland. Photograph: Luther Goldman.

Chesapeake Bay—A Good Place for Waterfowl

of habitat, and shoal waters where shellfish and submerged vegetation, important foods of waterfowl, are produced. It is the largest estuary in continental United States. The Bay is 165 nautical miles long, with a surface area of 4,300 square miles, and a shoreline of 4,500 miles. There are over fifty tributary rivers (1).

Because of its location midway between north and south and its predominantly salt and brackish water, the Bay remains largely unfrozen during most winters. This is important to the diving ducks, the canvasback (Figure 5), redhead, the scaups, scoters, and others that dive for clams, crustaceans, and submerged aquatic plants in the open waters of the Bay. The dabbling ducks (Figure 7), mallard, black, wigeon, teals, and other species that do much of their feeding on the surface or by tipping-up in the brackish marshes of the lower Eastern Shore of Maryland and Tidewater Virginia, and in the wild-rice marshes of the river estuaries, find an abundance of food provided by the seed-bearing plants of those habitats.

Adjacent to the marshes and shallow embayments of the Chesapeake are corn stubble fields, an important alternate feeding ground for Canada geese (Figure 8), whistling swans, and some of the dabbling ducks. The dramatic increase in Canada goose populations in the last twenty-five years has been in part due to residual grain left in the fields by the mechanical corn picker. This buildup of the goose population in the Bay area began with the establishment of federal, state, and private waterfowl refuges in the region. Blackwater National Wildlife Refuge, established in 1933, situated in southern Dorchester County, Maryland, was the first to attract geese in large numbers. The fourteen thousand-acre refuge has extensive marshes of Olney three-square, a favorite native food of geese, and grows various field crops and fescue grasses for the birds. In addition it is surrounded by grain stubble fields on private farmlands.

The approximately five percent of the corn crop left in the fields by the mechanical corn pickers on the Eastern Shore has "short-stopped" many geese and mallards that would otherwise be

Note: Numbers in parentheses are references to sources, beginning on page 203.

6

Figure 5. *Left, above,* Canvasbacks drifting along with the breeze at their backs. Note one bird beginning to dive and another stretching. Photograph: G. Michael Haramis, USFWS.

Figure 6. *Left, below,* John James Audubon's illustration of canvasbacks in Baltimore Harbor, circa 1830. From *Birds of America* by J. J. Audubon and J. B. Chevalier, 1840-1844.

Figure 7. *Above,* Wigeon or baldpate, coots, and a green-winged teal foraging together in a shallow pool. Note several wigeon "tipping-up" or "upending," typical feeding behavior of dabblers or puddle ducks. Photograph: E. O. Mellinger, USFWS.

continuing on to the Carolinas, Georgia, and Florida. In the early 1940s, Blackwater had a wintering population of five to ten thousand Canada geese. By the 1970s, one hundred thousand stopped off at the refuge and fifty to sixty thousand wintered there and in surrounding marshes and upland fields.

Because of the great increase in their population, Canada geese are now the number one waterfowl species in the hunter's bag in the Chesapeake. It was not always that way. In earlier years the canvasback was king of Chesapeake Bay waterfowl. It was the best eating and sporting duck and one of the handsomest. During its heyday no waterfowl species was more eagerly sought by the hunter, which helps explain one of the reasons for its decline.

The most famous hunting grounds for the canvasback were the Susquehanna Flats at the head of the Bay where submerged aquatic vegetation, particularly wild celery attracted these birds. In studying the canvasback biologists attribute the disappearance of the submerged aquatic vegetation as one of many factors causing the decline of that species. In the 1970s, canvasback populations did increase along the coastal sounds of North Carolina possibly due to better habitat conditions there as compared to the Bay. Since records have been maintained there were more canvasbacks in North Carolina in January 1980 for the first time than in Chesapeake Bay.

The great pioneer ornithologists Alexander Wilson and John James Audubon both wrote of the "lordly" canvasback. It was in Baltimore's outer harbor near the mouth of the Patapsco River and the present site of the Bethlehem Steel works at Sparrows Point that Audubon painted the canvasback portraits for his monumental work, the "Elephant Folio" edition of *The Birds of America*. The painting, made about 1830, shows three birds (Figure 6) with Fort McHenry, Baltimore Harbor, and the city in the background. Au-

Figure 8. *Right,* Canada geese in prime feeding site, the corn stubble. This scene is at the Blackwater National Wildlife Refuge. Photograph: Luther Goldman.

Waterfowl of the Chesapeake Bay Country

dubon's comments regarding his famous painting are noteworthy: "In the plate are represented two Males and a Female. In the background is a view of Baltimore, which I have had great pleasure in introducing on account of the hospitality which I have there experienced, and the generosity of its inhabitants, who on the occasion of a quantity of my plates having been destroyed by the mob during an outburst of political feeling, indemnified me for the loss."

So famous were the Susquehanna Flats canvasbacks and redheads as a gourmet food that each of the monarchs, Queen Victoria, King Edward, and King George, had standing orders for these ducks to be delivered in England every year.

2

The Species of Waterfowl of the Chesapeake Bay Country

Thirty-seven species of waterfowl (swans, geese, and ducks) have been reported from the Chesapeake Bay country. About three-fourths of these occur regularly. The others are rare or accidental—stragglers from western North America, the North Atlantic Coast of Canada, Great Britain, or Europe.

This great aggregation of waterfowl belongs to the avian family Anatidae (Latin for duck). Based on structure, plumage, and behavior, the species of Anatidae are divided into the following subfamilies: swans, geese, whistling or tree ducks, surface-feeding ducks, diving ducks, ruddy and masked ducks, and mergansers (2). In the swans and geese the sexes are similar in appearance, and both parents raise the offspring; as for the ducks, with the exception of the black duck, the females have a drabber plumage than the males, and only the female of most species raise the young.

The subfamily of swans is represented by the whistling swan, a North American native, and the introduced or exotic mute swan.

Waterfowl of the Chesapeake Bay Country

These are our largest waterfowl. The male mute swan weighs about twenty-five pounds, the male whistler about sixteen. The females of each species are a little smaller than the males. Swans feed much like the surface-feeding ducks, sometimes upending or extending the neck beneath the surface. The whistling swan also spends some time on land foraging in agricultural fields.

Our native swan is an abundant winter resident in Chesapeake Bay; whereas the mute swan, a native of Eurasia that has escaped from private estates, has only recently established itself in the area, and so far occurs only in small numbers. According to ornithologist Jan Reese, most of Chesapeake Bay's mute swans are centered in the lower estuaries of the Chester River, Eastern Bay, and the Choptank River. The mute swan is generally silent, but not "mute."

The subfamily of geese wintering in Chesapeake Bay include the Canada goose, snow goose, and Atlantic brant. There are numerous forms (subspecies or geographic races) of Canada geese (Figure 9) ranging in size (weight) from two to twelve pounds. They originate from breeding grounds in the far North, some from subarctic and arctic regions. The mid-Atlantic population that winters in the Chesapeake Bay area is mostly from the Hudson Bay and Ungava Peninsula area of Quebec. Most of these birds weigh about eight to nine pounds. The Canada goose population of Chesapeake Bay is the largest wintering unit of that species on the continent.

Two forms of snow geese occur in the general area of Chesapeake Bay. The greater snow goose winters along the Middle Atlantic Coast from about New Jersey to North Carolina. Some occur at Cape Charles near the mouth of the Bay. Where it occurs in the Chesapeake Bay area, the greater snow goose is indistinguishable from the lesser snow goose that is found in small numbers on the Eastern Shore of Maryland and sections of Tidewater Virginia.

The difference in size of the greater and lesser snow geese is not discernible in the field. They are discrete populations, coming from different breeding grounds in the arctic. However, the lesser snow has two color phases, white and blue (Figure 10). They were thought to be separate species (snow goose and blue goose) until found on the same breeding grounds and interbreeding. The

12

Figure 9. Most of the half million or so Canada geese that winter in the Chesapeake Bay country occur from about Kent County south into Dorchester County on the Eastern Shore of Maryland. Segments of the population also occur on the Western Shore and in Tidewater Virginia. Photograph: Luther Goldman.

14

greater snow goose male weighs about seven and one-half pounds, the lesser snow male averages about six pounds.

The Atlantic brant (Figure 11) is mainly a coastal bird, but a few occur in the lower Chesapeake Bay in the winter half of the year. Superficially, a brant looks like a small Canada goose. The male weighs an average of three and one-half pounds. Unlike the Canada and snow geese, brant seldom fly in a **V** formation, but usually in a loose line or abreast close to the water.

The surface-feeding ducks are also known as dabbling ducks, puddle ducks, shoal water ducks, marsh ducks, or river ducks. They feed on the surface by upending (also referred to as tipping-up); they usually occur in marshes, rivers, and shallow parts of bays; and several species also frequent grain stubble fields.

The mallard and black ducks (Figure 12 & 13) are the best known, most abundant, and largest of the surface-feeding ducks or dabblers. Their weights average about two and one-half pounds. The male mallard is known by its green head, hence the name "greenhead" applied to the species by many hunters. The black duck is well named because of its darkish plumage. It is readily identified in flight when overhead or when banking, by the silvery wing lining. The principal call of both species on the wintering ground is similar. Ralph S. Palmer, editor of the *Handbook of North American Birds*(3), states that the mallard is the ancestor of all domestic strains of ducks, except Muscovies.

The teals, blue-winged and green-winged, are our smallest ducks, and among the swiftest. The male green-winged teal averages about three-fourths of a pound; the male blue-winged teal, about one pound. Those who know waterfowl well can usually identify greenwings at a considerable distance by their characteristic flight. They swoop by in tight bunches, low over the water,

Figure 10. *Left, above,* Lesser snow geese, white and blue color phases. Photograph: Luther Goldman. Figure 11. *Left, below,* Brant feeding on algae at Chincoteague. Photograph: G. Michael Haramis, USFWS.

Figure 12. *Above,* Mallards are the most abundant ducks in North America and in the Chesapeake Bay country. The continental population approximates ten million. Photograph: Luther Goldman, USFWS.

Figure 13. *Right,* A black duck stretching and displaying the white or silvery underwing coverts that readily identify it in flight. Photograph: Luther Goldman, USFWS.

Figure 14. *Above,* Male and female blue-winged teals. This small surface-feeding duck or dabbler is one of the few native species of waterfowl of the Chesapeake Bay country. The center of the local breeding population is in the brackish marshes of Dorchester and Somerset counties. A few nest in similar habitats in Virginia marshes. Populations of this species from the northern breeding grounds begin to arrive in the Chesapeake's fresh tidal river marshes by the second half of August. Most of the local and transient populations winter in the Caribbean region and South America. Photograph: Allan D. Cruickshank.

Figure 15. *Right,* Pintails, mallards, and a male green-winged teal. Note the size of the teal, our smallest dabbling duck. Photograph: F. A. Heidelbauer, Iowa State Conservation Commission.

18

19

twisting and turning, then suddenly begin climbing, leveling off at a couple of hundred feet before dashing downward barely skimming the tops of the marsh grass. They wheel and turn like a flock of sandpipers in flight.

At hand, the male greenwing has a reddish head with a bright green eye-stripe. When the first bluewings and greenwings arrive in the Bay marshes from the north in late summer, they have not completed their molt and do not attain the bright plumage that they will have through the next breeding season until later in the autumn. The adult male blue-winged teal is known by the white facial mark or crescent (Figure 14) that appears in late fall, and in immature males in the winter. The drab colored females of both species are brownish.

Other surface-feeding or dabbling ducks are medium-sized, ranging in size between the mallard and the black duck on the one hand and the teals on the other. These ducks include the pintail (Figure 15) with its long central tail feathers; the shoveler (Figure 16) known by its spatulalike bill; the wigeon or baldpate (Figure 17) with its distinctive white crown; and the gadwall or gray duck (Figure 18) a rather nondescript bird that is difficult to distinguish in the field from a female mallard and some of the other female dabblers.

Figure 16. *Right, above,* The shoveler is a medium-sized duck with a spatulalike bill. The drake is strikingly marked—dark green head, white breast, rusty sides, and pale blue wing patch. The female's plumage is brownish, resembling the female mallard. The shoveler's favorite habitat in the Chesapeake Bay country is shallow ponds in brackish marshes. An unusual habitat where several thousand assemble in some winters is the dredge-fill area at Craney Island near Portsmouth, Virginia. Illustration: John W. Taylor. Figure 17. *Right, below,* Wigeon or baldpate (foreground) and canvasback. The wigeon, a surface-feeding duck or dabbler, sometimes snatches plants from the canvasback, a diving duck, when it surfaces with food following a dive. Photograph: Luther Goldman.

21

Figure 18. A gadwall or gray duck. The white wing patch on this grayish bird is a good field mark. Photograph: Matthew C. Perry, USFWS.

The Species of Waterfowl

With its conspicuous crest (Figure 19), the wood duck is one of our handsomest waterfowl species. It is well named because it spends much of its time in swamps and wooded stream bottoms and nests in holes in trees. It is a relative of the beautiful mandarin, a perching duck in Asia.

Most hunters know the wigeon and pintail in flight by their call notes. The wigeon's call is three whistling notes, with the middle note higher than the other two. The pintail's call is similar, but evenly pitched. The call of the wood duck is best known by the female's *oo-eek, oo-eek*. The male's call is a thin lisping whistle.

The diving ducks are composed of several groups, the pochards, which include the canvasback, redhead, greater and lesser scaups, and ring-necked duck. Other divers are the common goldeneye and bufflehead, sometimes called bay ducks; the sea ducks, the white-winged, surf, and black scoters; and the oldsquaw. Other species of diving ducks that occasionally occur in Chesapeake Bay are the eiders and the harlequin duck.

The diving ducks have large feet, with a lobed hind toe, and short legs that are farther to the rear of the body than in the dabbling or surface-feeding ducks. Thus, they are better equipped for diving and swimming beneath the surface but are awkward on land and do not visit crop fields like the mallard, black duck, and pintail. Some of the divers use their wings to help them maneuver while under water. Because their feet are placed closer to the rear of their bodies, they can not rise vertically from the water like the dabblers, but have to paddle along the water for a considerable distance before rising (Figure 20).

Some of the divers, particularly the canvasback and scaups, often assemble in large rafts that may occasionally number twenty-five thousand birds. Smaller numbers of redheads may be mixed in these rafts. A characteristic of many large canvasback rafts is the so-called "fish hook" formation—a line of birds strung out with a slight turn at one end (Figure 21).

When they take to the air, divers can often be identified by their flight formations. The flight of the canvasback is direct, without the dipping and weaving of the scaups, and usually in a loose **V** formation. The scoters customarily fly close to the water and often in a single line.

24

The canvasback is the best known of the diving ducks of Chesapeake Bay. It is one of the largest ducks. The average weight of the male canvasback is about two and three quarters pounds, with some males weighing up to three and one-half pounds. The average weights of the female canvasback and male redhead are about two and one-half pounds; with the average for the female redhead, about two pounds.

The canvasback is one of the fastest flying ducks. When it gains momentum, the canvasback can pitch downward past a duck blind at seventy miles per hour. Its unique profile, streamlined in flight, is accentuated more when it is at rest. Looking at the bird from a right angle, one is taken by the striking appearance of its wedge-shaped head (Figure 22).

The scaups (Figure 23) are better known in the Chesapeake Bay country as blackheads or bluebills. The male greater scaup has a green tinted head, the male lesser scaup, a purplish tinted head. In flight they are best distinguished by the more extended white wing stripe of the greater scaup.

The wedge-shaped head of the canvasback immediately sets it apart from its look-alike, the redhead (Figure 24) which is easily distinguished at close range by its round head and abrupt forehead.

The ring-necked duck (Figure 25) resembles the scaup, but the head of the male has an angular shape and is held more erect. The brownish ring at the base of the neck of the male is not easily seen. However, the ring on the bill stands out and is a good field mark.

Figure 19. *Left, above,* Drake wood ducks. They occur in marshes and wooded bottoms. Wood ducks are one of four species of "native" waterfowl that regularly nest in the Chesapeake Bay country. Others like the Canada goose and mallard are not native nesters, but have been imprinted or introduced to the area. Photograph: E. O. Mellinger, USFWS. Figure 20. *Left, below,* Most diving ducks, like this canvasback, run splashing along the surface as they take off in flight. The dabblers or puddle ducks, whose legs are not placed as close to the rear of their bodies, can rise almost straight up or vertically from the water. Photograph: Matthew C. Perry, USFWS.

26

Figure 21. *Left, above,* "Fishhook" formation of canvasbacks, a characteristic of that species when forming huge rafts. Photograph: Matthew C. Perry, USFWS. Figure 22. *Left, below,* Profile of a female canvasback. Photograph: G. Michael Haramis, USFWS.

Figure 23. *Above,* Female, *above,* and male greater scaups caught in banding traps. Scaups are better known to duck hunters as bluebills or blackheads. Photograph: G. Michael Haramis, USFWS.

27

Waterfowl of the Chesapeake Bay Country

Perhaps ring-billed duck would have been a more appropriate name. The ringneck swims higher or more upright on the water than the other divers. In contrast to the brackish and salt waters of the Bay where most of the scaups, redheads, and canvasbacks are seen, ringnecks occur more on wooded ponds and in fresh water and are relatively uncommon in winter in the Chesapeake area, being seen mostly during migration to and from the more southerly wintering grounds.

The male common goldeneye and male bufflehead are chunky ducks with black and white plumage patterns and generally occur in the same habitats, the brackish and salt bays. The common goldeneye has a round white spot below the eye (Figure 26); the bufflehead, a large white patch on its green head (Figure 27). The bufflehead is one of the smallest ducks. The average weights of males and females are a little over a pound and half a pound respectively. Buffleheads and common goldeneyes do not form large rafts like canvasbacks and scaups but are usually seen as singles or very small groups. The goldeneye, a little larger than the bufflehead, is better known in the Chesapeake Bay country as "whistler," from the sound made by its rapidly beating wings; the bufflehead, as "butterball," from its small chunky appearance. Buffleheads rise quickly from the water, more like dabblers.

Figure 24a. *Right, above left,* The canvasback's look-alike, the redhead (in flight), has a rounder head and lighter bill. Photograph: Luther Goldman, USFWS. Figure 24b. *Right, above right,* Illustration: Bob Hines, USFWS. Figure 25. *Right, below,* The ring-necked duck resembles the scaup, but the head of the male has an angular shape and is held more erect. The ring-neck swims higher or more upright in the water than the other divers. Photograph: S. A. Grimes.

SCAUP

REDHEAD

CANVASBACK

Figure 26. The circular white patch at the base of the bill identifies the male common goldeneye or whistler. Photograph: G. Michael Haramis, USFWS.

Figure 27. The white wedge-shaped patch on the head of the male bufflehead is a diagnostic field mark of this smallest diving duck. Photograph: G. Michael Haramis, USFWS.

The scoters (Figure 28), known to the hunting fraternity as sea ducks or sea coots, are salt water birds. They are generally associated with large bodies of water and are more abundant in the oceanic littoral zone and coastal embayments than in Chesapeake Bay. However, all are fairly common in the Bay. They are not eagerly sought by the hunters as they are not as good eating as most other ducks. The white-winged scoter is the largest of the sea ducks and easiest to identify, especially in flight. The male averages three and one-half pounds, with some weighing four pounds. It is fairly easy to pick out scoters in flight by their dark color and coarse looking heads and necks, and because they often fly in a line, usually low over the water.

The oldsquaw or "south southerly," (Figure 29) as it was known to the oldtime hunters, is also a sea duck and is a handsome bird with a long tail like the pintail. The soft melodious call during the winter is unique among the waterfowl; and with the advent of spring seems continuous for long periods. According to J.C. Phillips (4), the local name "south southerly" suggests the several syllables of the call.

The ruddy duck (Figure 30), also a diver, belongs to the stiff-tailed subfamily of waterfowl. It is one of the easiest ducks to

Figure 28. *Left, above,* As they are generally associated with large bodies of water, the white-winged scoter, *above,* and the other two species of scoter in the Chesapeake Bay country are known as bay or sea ducks. Some, however, wander up the Potomac as far as the District of Columbia, and some into the Patapsco to Baltimore Harbor, as well as in other river estuaries. Illustration: John W. Taylor.
Figure 29. *Left, below,* Like the white-winged scoter, the oldsquaw is also known as a bay or sea duck, and occurs in the broader waters of the Chesapeake and along the coast. The male has a long tail like the pintail, a river and marsh duck. Illustration: John W. Taylor.

34

Figure 30. *Left,* The ruddy duck is easily identified by its plumpness, large white face patch, and uptilted tail. Photograph: Luther Goldman.

Figure 31. *Above,* Heads of male mergansers, *left to right,* hooded, red-breasted, and common. Illustration: John W. Taylor.

36

identify at a distance, as it usually swims with an up-tilted tail, and both sexes have a large white face patch. Ruddies are generally seen in large flocks and most often in brackish sections of our large rivers. More recently, however, many have occurred in fresh water areas near cities such as Washington, D.C., Baltimore, and Philadelphia.

The three species of mergansers, common, hooded (Figure 31), and red-breasted, have serrated bills, modified for catching fish. Except for the male common merganser, they are also known by their crested heads. The common and hooded occur more in fresh and brackish water, the red-breasted, in salt water.

Among the rarer waterfowl of the Bay are the common and king eiders, and the harlequin duck. A few are seen in most winters, predominantly in the lower Bay. A good vantage point for viewing these three more northern wintering birds is the Chesapeake Bay Bridge-Tunnel that leads from Norfolk, Virginia, to Cape Charles on the Eastern Shore of Virginia.

Barrow's goldeneye, a bird of the North Pacific and North Atlantic in winter and rarely seen south of Massachusetts at that season, was reported on the Christmas Count in the lower Chester River in 1979. Only three have ever been reported from Maryland and apparently none from Virginia. Barrow's goldeneye has a crescent-shaped white spot between the bill and the eye, as opposed to the round white spot of the common goldeneye.

The fulvous whistling duck (formerly fulvous tree duck) (Figure 32) is a rare visitor from the Gulf Coast region. Some nest in the Louisiana and Texas rice fields. Until recent years it was unknown

Figure 32. *Left,* Fulvous whistling duck, a rare bird from the Louisiana and Texas Coast has been appearing intermittently in small numbers in the Chesapeake Bay area in the last ten years. Fifteen were reported at Blackwater National Wildlife Refuge on November 4, 1977; and twenty-four at Eastern Neck National Wildlife Refuge in November 1979. There are also reports of its occurrence at Ocean City, Maryland, and Sandy Point State Park near Annapolis. The neck and legs of this species are longer than those of other ducks. Photograph: Brooke Meanley.

to the Chesapeake Bay area, where it was first reported in Virginia in 1960. The fulvous whistling duck has a longer neck and longer legs than the other ducks.

The white-fronted goose, associated mainly with the more western flyways, occasionally shows up among a Canada goose concentration at Blackwater Refuge or some other area in the Chesapeake Bay country.

Accidental wanderers from Europe or Great Britain are the Eurasian wigeon, tufted duck, and common pochard; and from the West Indies, the masked duck.

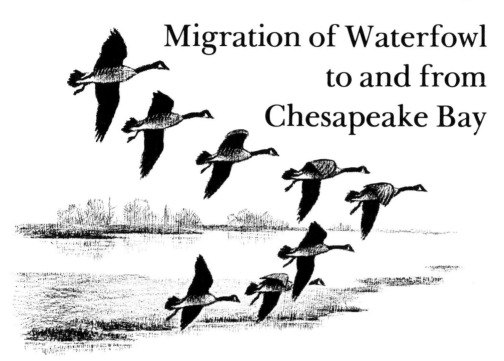

3

Migration of Waterfowl
to and from
Chesapeake Bay

Most waterfowl that winter in Chesapeake Bay are produced in Canada. Others come from Alaska, and some from as far north as Greenland. The larger waterfowl, swans, geese, and brant, as a group, nest farther north than most of the ducks. While some ducks are produced on the Arctic tundra, most that winter in Chesapeake Bay are from the prairie pothole country of North Dakota, southern Saskatchewan, and Manitoba, and a scattering of localities across eastern Canada and the northern tier of states.

In migrating to the Chesapeake, waterfowl follow well established routes. F.C. Lincoln of the U.S. Biological Survey divided migratory patterns of birds into four major flyways: Atlantic (Figure 33), Mississippi, Central, and Pacific. Lincoln's concept was based on waterfowl banding records preceding 1935. This division of the migratory routes is still conveniently used in a broad sense. Using the censuses on breeding and wintering grounds and along the routes of migration, in conjunction with a great wealth of data from visual observations and banding records, accumulated since 1935, Frank Bellrose, of the Illinois Natural History Survey, was able to define the migratory routes more specifically for separate species of waterfowl. Bellrose proposed the use of the term corridor rather than flyways or routes (5):

> I believe a route represents a path only a mile or two wide which waterfowl follow consistently from year to year. Each corridor, on the other hand, consists of a web of routes, some of which may cross or crisscross within a single corridor. The corridors do not have sharp boundaries; rather there may be gradual changes from the center of a flight corridor to its margin in the numbers of waterfowl using it.

The corridor along which the greatest variety or number of species move toward Chesapeake Bay originates in the southern prairie provinces of Canada, the "pothole country," or "duck factory" as it is often referred to by waterfowl biologists. Species using this corridor in greatest numbers are the canvasback (Figure 34), redhead, wigeon, mallard, pintail, blue-winged teal, and northern shoveler. There are spur routes that depart slightly from the main path, but in general the corridor leads southeastward from the Canadian and North Dakota prairies to the Great Lakes, a favorite rest area; and from there across the Alleghenys to Chesapeake Bay. Whistling swans migrating from breeding grounds in Alaska and the Arctic coast of western Canada follow the last leg of this corridor after a long journey across Alberta and Saskatchewan, and an occasional stopover at Devils Lake, North Dakota (see Figure 35). Greater scaups that breed in some of the same sections of Alaska as the swans, fly in an almost direct line, east southeast to Chesapeake Bay. Whistling swans and canvasbacks usually arrive in the Bay around the same time.

The half million Canada geese wintering in Chesapeake Bay follow a corridor originating from breeding grounds in northern Quebec, particularly the Ungava Peninsula and the east side of Hudson Bay. They follow the east coast of Hudson Bay almost due south to the Finger Lakes region of central New York and then through eastern Pennsylvania to the head of Chesapeake Bay (Figure 36). In migration they usually fly at an average of two to three

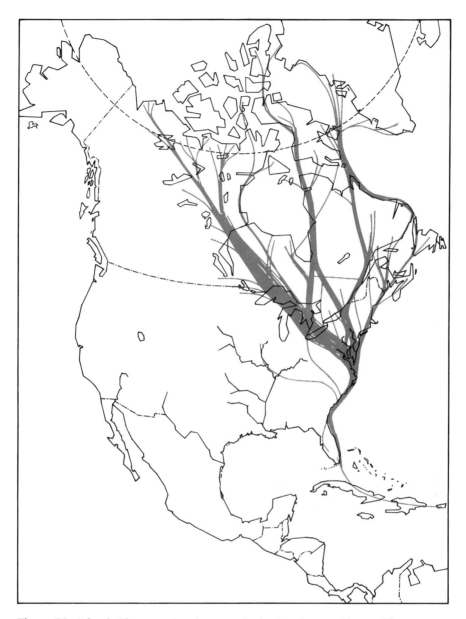

Figure 33. Atlantic Flyway and major waterfowl migration corridors to Chesapeake Bay. Illustration: Bob Hines, USFWS.

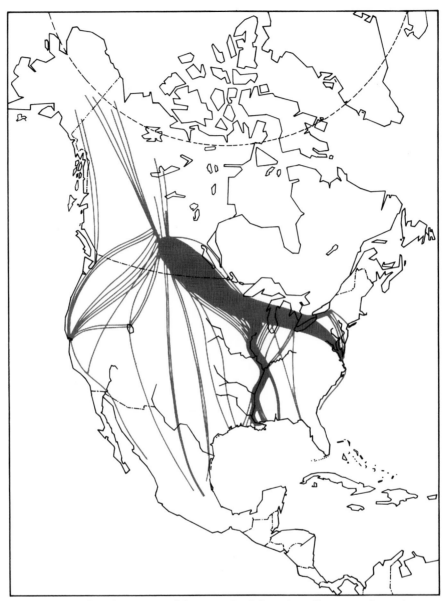

Figure 34. Migration routes of the canvasback from breeding grounds to winter-ing grounds. Heaviest flight is to Chesapeake Bay. Illustration: Bob Hines, USFWS.

Figure 35. Main migration corridor of the whistling swan from breeding grounds in northern Alaska and northwestern Canadian tundra to Chesapeake Bay wintering area. USFWS.

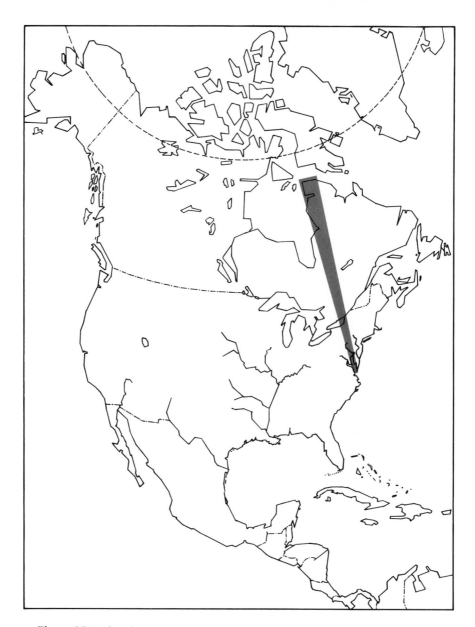

Figure 36. Main migration corridor between nesting and wintering grounds of the Mid-Atlantic population of Canada geese. USFWS.

thousand feet; with altitudes increasing over higher terrain. Canada goose families leave the breeding grounds together in the fall, and continue together during the winter in aggregations of families. Snow geese and whistling swans also remain together in winter as family units. Biologists use these family groups on the wintering areas to obtain an estimate of the annual productivity of these species.

In recent years, a small population of lesser snow geese (white and blue phases) have wintered in the Chesapeake Bay country (Figure 37). Segments of that population are often seen at Blackwater National Wildlife Refuge and in the Kent County section of the upper Eastern Shore of Maryland. A map in the *Handbook of North American Birds* (3) shows the lesser snow geese coming from Baffin Island, which lies between the north end of Hudson Bay and Greenland. These geese appear to follow the same migration path as Canada geese destined for Chesapeake Bay and may migrate along with them. They often mingle with the Canadas at Blackwater and elsewhere in the Chesapeake area.

Atlantic brant, some of which nest in northern Greenland (farther north than any bird in the world) and in the Canadian arctic archipelago, follow the Hudson Bay corridor for a part of the way south in the fall (Figure 38). Frank Bellrose indicates that many brant stop over at a staging area in James Bay at the south end of Hudson Bay, and from there some of them make a direct flight to the New York City area, where a great many assemble at nearby Barnegat Bay, New Jersey; some then disperse down the coast south to the vicinity of the mouth of Chesapeake Bay (5).

The oldsquaw nests in the arctic, farther north than virtually any other duck. According to Palmer in the *Handbook of North American Birds* (3): "Many Oldsquaws do not migrate until the land is frozen and the ice is forming on the sea. In general, they are gone from land areas in northern portions of their breeding range by early September at the very latest." Some winter along the southwest coast of Greenland and off Newfoundland, or as far north as there is unfrozen water.

Those black ducks that are widely dispersed in the northeast during the nesting season, follow a number of routes to their major

Figure 37. Lesser snow geese rising from crop stubble field. Photograph: Luther Goldman.

wintering ground in Chesapeake Bay marshes and shallow embayments. Lincoln reports on one that is rather devious (6):

> Black ducks, mallards, and blue-winged teals that have gathered in southern Ontario during the fall leave these feeding grounds and proceed southwest over a course that is apparently headed for the Mississippi Valley. Many do continue this route down the Ohio Valley, but others, upon reaching the St. Clair Flats between Michigan and Ontario, swing abruptly to the southeast and cross the mountains to reach the Atlantic coast south of New Jersey. This route with its Mississippi Valley branch, has been fully documented by the recovery records of ducks banded at Lake Scugog, Ontario (Figure 39).

From band recoveries, it appears that most green-winged teals that migrate through or winter in the Chesapeake Bay country, like the black duck, originate from breeding grounds in the Canadian maritimes: New Brunswick, Nova Scotia, Quebec, Newfoundland, and Labrador.

The migration of the canvasback from its major breeding grounds in the prairie pothole country to the Chesapeake Bay and other parts of its winter range is better known than the migratory habits of most waterfowl species. Following the molting period in late summer, when canvasbacks and other waterfowl are flightless for about a month, the first birds from the major Canadian breeding grounds begin to move into the northern Great Plains. This movement southward into North Dakota begins in early September. Their numbers build up through October, with most of them having passed through the northern plains by early November. At Delta, Manitoba, heartland of the canvasback breeding grounds, H. Albert Hochbaum (7) states:

> Although the early autumn flights accompany north winds, weather does not influence the mass departure southward from the Delta Marsh. Come ice, snow and strong winds, or mild Indian summer weather, the Delta Canvasbacks always leave in a body for southern waters in mid-October. After the middle of the month the species is uncommon.

Hochbaum further states that unlike some of the mallards and lesser scaups, canvasbacks in Manitoba leave two or three weeks

47

before the bays are frozen. Some mallards and lesser scaups stay as long as they can find open water.

Some male canvasbacks begin moving toward the wintering grounds first but may be passed over by females that tend to migrate farther south and greater distances. Hochbaum states as follows, "I believe that most of the adult males move southward directly from the molting lakes, not to join the young birds and the old hens until they reach the wintering waters."

Although most canvasbacks destined for Chesapeake Bay come from the southern Canadian prairies and North Dakota, banding studies have shown that a few come from as far as the Bering Sea Coast of Alaska. J.G. King banded fifty adult canvasbacks at Takslesluk Lake near the Bering Sea Coast in 1964. From those banded on August 8, there have been seven widely distributed recoveries: California (three), Texas Gulf Coast, Minnesota, Michigan, and Maryland (one each).

After they leave Canada and the Dakotas, canvasbacks congregate in great numbers along the upper Mississippi River in October and early November. In recent years they have been using several navigational pools in the river. The two most important pools are at LaCrosse, Wisconsin and Keokuk, Iowa. Populations of one hundred thousand sometimes are seen on one of these pools. They spend three or four weeks there feeding on an abundance of fingernail clams, wild celery, and other wetland plants before taking off for the Chesapeake and other wintering areas in the eastern half of the United States.

The eastern population of canvasbacks, most of which seems to stop off at LaCrosse, follows a route to Chesapeake Bay that takes it to the Detroit area and nearby Lake St. Clair; then to Lake Erie and southeastward across the Appalachians to the Bay. A segment of this flight moves farther eastward from Lake Erie to the Finger Lakes of central New York before dropping down to Chesapeake Bay. As long as the Finger Lakes remain unfrozen, a few canvasbacks linger there for some time and may even spend the winter. On Cayuga Lake near Ithaca, Arthur A. Allen found that males usually exceeded females at a ratio of four or five to one; and in some flocks there may be twenty-five males and one female (8). This

48

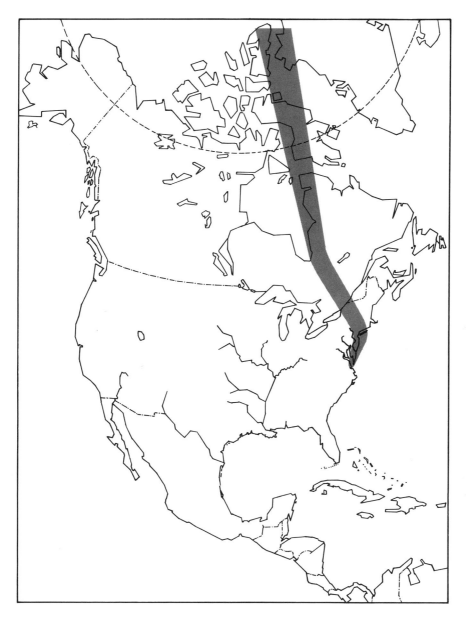

Figure 38. Migration route of the Atlantic brant from breeding grounds along the
northern Greenland coast, Ellesmere Island, and Baffin Island to wintering
grounds along the Middle Atlantic Coast. USFWS.

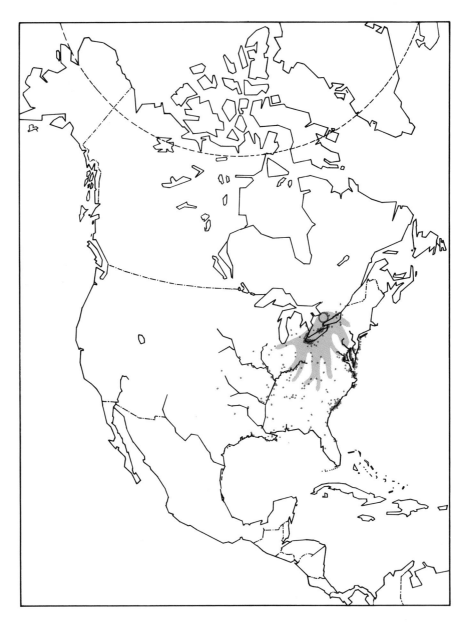

Figure 39. Dispersal of black ducks banded at Lake Scugog, Ontario, in the fall and recovered in passage and on wintering grounds. Note concentration of recoveries in Chesapeake Bay. From C. E. Addy, USFWS.

50

uneven sex ratio is due in part to male canvasbacks migrating separately from females, and some males taking a more northerly route to the Middle Atlantic Coastal region. Also, more males are found in the northern part of the winter range. Furthermore, there is a disparate sex ratio favoring males in the general population.

Other migratory flights of canvasbacks move south of Minnesota and Iowa down the Mississippi Valley to the Gulf Coast. Farther west, most of the birds from breeding grounds in Alaska, British Columbia, and Alberta migrate to western wintering grounds, with a few going to Mexico. San Francisco Bay is the most important wintering ground of western canvasback populations.

Canvasbacks arrive at Chesapeake Bay later than most of the other ducks. The surface-feeding or dabbling ducks are the earliest, a few moving in by early August. The blue-winged teal is usually the first of the dabblers to appear. They begin showing up in August in some of the fresh tidal river marshes. The incoming flight of the first green-winged teals follows about a week later. At this time during August and early September, the two species of teals and the wood duck, many of the latter of which breed locally, are the waterfowl of the ripening wild rice marshes. The first shovelers arrive soon after the teals, in late August.

The larger dabblers, the American wigeon, mallard, black duck, and pintail begin to arrive in Chesapeake Bay in early September, with a peak migration period from early October to the middle of November. Fred Scott, a Virginia ornithologist, reported 500 pintails on September 30, 1979, at Hopewell on the upper James River, a few miles south of Richmond. A few Canada geese arrive in late September, but the main flight is in October and November, at the time of the arrival of most of the diving ducks and whistling swans.

Waterfowl coming in on the fall flight often arrive at the Chesapeake in successive waves during a relatively short period. On October 3, 1976, the mass arrival of Canada geese was spectacular, as reported in *Maryland Birdlife* (9):

> Nearly every observer from Frederick County eastward reported flock after flock, all day long and continuing into the night. Jo Solem claimed Oct. 3 was the best day for migration

Waterfowl of the Chesapeake Bay Country

"I've had in eight years we've been in Howard County"; she counted 35 flocks of Canada Geese most containing 30 to 50 birds, flying southeastward over her home between 1:15 and 3:15 p.m.; and in the evening she stepped outside every 15 minutes between 7 and 8:15 p.m. and heard 1 or 2 flocks each time. Dorothy Rauth counted a total of 1,676 geese over Fulton, also in Howard County. At Germantown, Robert Warfield counted 29 flocks with about 75 birds per flock between 11:35 a.m. and midnight, and estimated between 2,000 and 3,500 geese over his home in a 20-hour period. At Beltsville, Bill Hayes counted 1,930 geese in 50 flocks. Mike Resch's estimate of 10,000-12,000 over his Parkville home agrees closely with Hal Wierenga's total of 11,500 flying past Sandy Point.

A few canvasbacks appear in the Bay in October, increasing in numbers through November, with a peak from about November 15 to December 15. John W. Taylor who lives on Selby Bay off the lower South River below Annapolis says that canvasbacks usually arrive there after Thanksgiving. Frank C. Kirkwood, Maryland's pioneer ornithologist, reported in his book, *A List of the Birds of Maryland* (10), that a large number of canvasbacks in company with redheads and blackheads (scaups) were present on the lower Gunpowder River as early as October 3 (1889).

In former years, canvasbacks arriving on the fall flight in the Bay settled at first on the Susquehanna Flats and other sections of the upper Bay, the Bush, Gunpowder, and Middle River estuaries. They were attracted to the great beds of wild celery that formerly flourished in the fresher water sections of the Bay. Old time hunters often reported several hundred thousand canvasbacks on the Flats in December. By late December and in January with the freeze-ups in the shallow freshwater estuaries (Figure 40), and heavy shooting, birds moved south to the middle and lower Bay sections; with lesser numbers moving to Back Bay (below Norfolk) and Currituck Sound, North Carolina.

Robert E. Stewart, waterfowl biologist in the U.S. Fish and Wildlife Service, described a tremendous flight of canvasbacks arriving on the Susquehanna Flats at the end of their fall migration from the northwest. He witnessed this mass arrival in the 1950s at

52

Figure 40. Canvasbacks on an icy section of Chesapeake Bay, January 1978.
Photograph: G. Michael Haramis, USFWS.

the time he was conducting his five-year survey of Chesapeake Bay waterfowl (11). Stewart explained that during the three hours he watched this incoming flight, the birds came from a very high altitude, appearing to be dropping out of the clouds. As they dropped down from tremendous heights in bands of two and three hundred birds, "they came roaring by like an express train." Band after band continued dropping onto the Flats until well over one hundred thousand birds had settled in. Bob surmised that most of the birds had probably come from the St. Clair Flats opposite Detroit direct to the Susquehanna Flats, because he had heard that just previous to this incoming flight, about one hundred thousand canvasbacks had moved out of Lake St. Clair.

In the late 1970s, G. Michael Haramis witnessed the arrival of migrating canvasbacks in the Gibson Island area near Annapolis. There was a strong northwest wind, and as Haramis noted they were "dropping out of the clouds" all afternoon. They were riding a tail wind; coming in on a hard cold front.

In 1924, William Brewster, the New England ornithologist, wrote of a large migrating flock of black scoters that came tumbling out of the sky at a great height (12).

> After circling or doubling for two or three minutes without perceptibly lowering their flight, the birds were accustomed to descend neither spirally nor on long inclines, but *almost vertically*, and with such velocity that the eye could scarcely follow them, making a rushing sound not unlike that of a strong wind blowing through pine tops, but perhaps still more like that of escaping steam. It could be heard distinctly more than a mile away, and I was sometimes awakened by it at daybreak, when sleeping in a tent by the lake shore.

Brewster stated that the scoters kept their wings tightly closed until within 100 feet or less of the water.

A spectacular flight of migrating waterfowl moving along the Middle Atlantic Coast toward the wintering grounds was noted on October 17, 1970, by Ed Addy, waterfowl biologist with the U.S. Fish and Wildlife Service. Addy was at Bethany Beach, Delaware where he observed a massive southward flight of scoters. Flocks passing by were estimated to total over a million birds. Most of the

54

scoters were probably heading for offshore waters along the southern Delmarva Coast or the lower part of Chesapeake Bay.

Many ducks continue south after a brief stop-over at the Bay. Most blue-winged teals, abundant during the early southward migration, continue on to the West Indies and South America. The blue-winged teal winters farther south in greater numbers than most other North American waterfowl. Because of the long journey back north in the spring, bluewings are usually the last waterfowl to move through the Chesapeake Bay country on the northward flight.

Spring migration to the breeding ground for most waterfowl is over the same routes followed in the fall. In mild winters, some Canada geese and mallards are moving northward in early February, on the first southerly winds of spring. However, most waterfowl depart from the Bay in late February and during March.

The migration of the geese and swans are the most spectacular. Migrating during the day and night, their trumpeting calls are heard at a great distance as they fly along in the familiar **V** formations. A flock of eighty migrating swans that I observed over Laurel, Maryland in mid-March was accompanied by six ring-billed gulls, a smaller species, flying in a **V** within the larger **V** of the swans. I have never heard of this before. Swans migrating to the breeding grounds fly by way of the Great Lakes, which is also the route of the ring-billed gulls.

Dr. William Sladen of Johns Hopkins University has charted the migration of whistling swans from Chesapeake Bay toward their arctic breeding grounds. With the use of aircraft, he has followed swans that he fitted with radio tracking transmitters, from the Bay to the Great Lakes, then to Minnesota and North Dakota, into Saskatchewan. Presumably he lost them from that point as they continued toward the arctic (13).

In some years, canvasbacks begin moving to the breeding grounds as early as the last week in February. However, the peak flight from the Bay is between March 1 and March 30. Most canvasbacks are still on the Chesapeake wintering grounds by the end of the first week in March. At that time, in early March 1979, there were at several places that I visited as many canvasbacks as I had

Figure 41. Lesser scaup, also known as bluebill and blackhead. Photograph: E. O. Mellinger.

seen in the same places during mid-winter; an estimated six thousand in the Chesapeake Bay Bridge area between Bay Ridge and Gibson Island; three thousand in Baltimore Harbor; five thousand off Pope's Creek along the Virginia section of the Potomac; two thousand off Persimmon Point, King George County, Virginia section of the Potomac; five hundred at the mouth of Currioman Bay, Potomac River; and two thousand on the section of South River below Annapolis. When I checked the Pope's Creek, Virginia area on April 19, 1979, there were no canvasbacks present, but there were an estimated three thousand lesser scaups (Figure 41). The scaups are known to migrate later than most canvasbacks.

Close to the time of departure from the Chesapeake, local wintering waterfowl and birds arriving from the South Atlantic area stage at various points along the Bay, as these congregations build up to several thousand birds in some instances. Although most waterfowl depart from the Bay in March, there are still many thousands passing through and leaving the Chesapeake in April and a few thousand in early May.

Local ornithologists have reported on many such congregations, their data having appeared in *Maryland Birdlife* and other ornithological literature. The following records from the 1970s and early 1980s are of interest:

7,000 whistling swans near Queenstown, Maryland, March 14, 1980 (B. Meanley)

10,000 scoters and 500 red-breasted mergansers, South River, March 25, 1978 (H. Wierenga)

12,000 lesser scaups at the mouth of the Gunpowder River, March 30, 1978 (R. Ringler)

1,000 oldsquaws in Talbot County, April 1, 1975 (H. Armistead)

600 blue-winged teals, southern Dorchester County, April 6, 1975 (H. Armistead)

700 green-winged teals, southern Dorchester County, April 6, 1975 (H. Armistead)

400 red-breasted mergansers, South River, April 9, 1977 (H. Wierenga)

25,000 white-winged scoters, Sharp's Island, Talbot County, April 22, 1976 (J. Reese)

1,075 white-winged scoters off Sandy Point (near Annapolis), May 3, 1975 (H. Wierenga)

Waterfowl of the Chesapeake Bay Country

Blue-winged teals, usually the latest migrants, are still passing through the Chesapeake Bay country in late April and early May. In the agricultural sections of Maryland and Virginia, they are often seen in "wet weather" ponds or puddles in low places in corn stubble fields or in more permanent ponds. In the shallow ponds there are frequently a number of migrating shorebirds, particularly lesser yellowlegs, solitary sandpipers, least sandpipers, and common snipe.

A few Atlantic brant are usually present along the Delmarva coast in May. In the middle of May 1978, John W. Taylor and I saw at least five hundred in the Chincoteague Bay and Gargathy Bay sections of Accomack County Virginia. In the same area, I have also seen a few able-bodied brant flying about in June. Perhaps they never left the area.

Migration of Waterfowl

FALL MIGRATION SCHEDULE
(Chesapeake Bay)

	Normal Period	Peak
Whistling Swan	Oct. 15-Dec. 5	Oct. 25-Nov. 30
Canada Goose	Sept. 15-Dec. 30	Oct. 15-Nov. 15
Atlantic Brant	Oct. 15-Dec. 15	Nov. 1-Dec. 10
Greater Snow Goose	Oct. 15-Dec. 15	Nov. 10-Dec. 15
Mallard	Sept. 15-Dec. 15	Oct. 15-Dec. 10
Black Duck	Sept. 10-Dec. 15	Oct. 15-Dec. 5
Gadwall	Sept. 1-Dec. 10	Oct. 15-Nov. 20
Pintail	Sept. 1-Dec. 15	Oct. 20-Nov. 30
Green-winged Teal	Aug. 20-Dec. 15	Oct. 15-Nov. 30
Blue-winged Teal	Aug. 15-Nov. 15	Sept. 1-Oct. 15
American Wigeon	Sept. 10-Dec. 10	Oct. 10-Nov. 30
Northern Shoveler	Aug. 25-Dec. 15	Sept. 20-Nov. 15
Wood Duck	Aug. 15-Nov. 15	Sept. 1-Nov. 1
Redhead	Oct. 10-Dec. 20	Nov. 5-Dec. 15
Ring-necked Duck	Oct. 10-Dec. 10	Oct. 20-Dec. 5
Canvasback	Oct. 15-Dec. 15	Nov. 15-Dec. 15
Greater Scaup	Oct. 1-Dec. 1	Nov. 10-Dec. 5
Lesser Scaup	Sept. 25-Dec. 15	Nov. 10-Dec. 15
Common Goldeneye	Oct. 15-Dec. 15	Nov. 10-Dec. 15
Bufflehead	Oct. 15-Dec. 20	Nov. 1-Dec. 5
Oldsquaw	Oct. 20-Dec. 15	Nov. 5-Dec. 10
White-winged Scoter	Oct. 5-Dec. 10	Oct. 20-Dec. 5
Surf Scoter	Oct. 1-Dec. 10	Oct. 15-Dec. 5
Black Scoter	Sept. 15-Nov. 30	Oct. 10-Nov. 15
Ruddy Duck	Sept. 20-Dec. 10	Oct. 15-Dec. 10
Hooded Merganser	Oct. 1-Dec. 10	Oct. 25-Dec. 10
Common Merganser	Oct. 15-Dec. 15	Nov. 15-Dec. 15
Red-breasted Merganser	Oct. 15-Dec. 15	Nov. 1-Dec. 5

Note: Data from *Birds of Maryland and the District of Columbia* (1958), *Maryland Birdlife*, and the author's notes.

Waterfowl of the Chesapeake Bay Country

SPRING MIGRATION SCHEDULE
(Chesapeake Bay)

	Normal Period	Peak
Whistling Swan	Feb. 25-Apr. 30	Mar. 10-Apr. 1
Canada Goose	Feb. 15-Apr. 30	Mar. 1-Apr. 1
Atlantic Brant	Feb. 20-May 1	Mar. 1-Apr. 15
Greater Snow Goose	Feb. 20-Mar. 30	Feb. 20-Mar. 15
Mallard	Feb. 10-May 15	Feb. 20-Mar. 25
Black Duck	Feb. 15-Apr. 30	Feb. 25-Mar. 30
Gadwall	Mar. 10-Apr. 30	Mar. 15-Apr. 15
Pintail	Feb. 1-May 1	Feb. 20-Mar. 20
Green-winged Teal	Feb. 25-May 5	Mar. 5-Apr. 15
Blue-winged Teal	Mar. 15-May 20	Apr. 1-May 10
American Wigeon	Mar. 1-May 15	Mar. 15-Apr. 15
Northern Shoveler	Mar. 1-May 15	Mar. 15-Apr. 30
Wood Duck	Feb. 15-Apr. 30	Mar. 1-Apr. 1
Redhead	Mar. 1-May 1	Mar. 15-Apr. 15
Ring-necked Duck	Feb. 15-May 1	Mar. 1-Apr. 10
Canvasback	Feb. 20-May 1	Mar. 1-Mar. 30
Greater Scaup	Mar. 1-May 15	Mar. 15-Apr. 15
Lesser Scaup	Mar. 1-May 15	Mar. 15-Apr. 15
Common Goldeneye	Mar. 1-Apr. 30	Mar. 15-Apr. 15
Bufflehead	Mar. 1-Apr. 30	Mar. 15-Apr. 15
Oldsquaw	Mar. 5-Apr. 30	Mar. 15-Apr. 15
White-winged Scoter	Mar. 15-May 1	Mar. 25-Apr. 25
Surf Scoter	Feb. 20-May 10	Mar. 1-Apr. 30
Black Scoter	Feb. 20-May 10	Feb. 25-Apr. 30
Ruddy Duck	Mar. 1-May 10	Mar. 15-Apr. 15
Hooded Merganser	Feb. 20-May 10	Mar. 10-Apr. 30
Common Merganser	Feb. 20-May 10	Mar. 5-Apr. 30
Red-breasted Merganser	Mar. 10-May 15	Mar. 25-Apr. 30

60

4

The Waterfowl's Environment

I n late summer when the first blue-winged teals arrive in the
Chesapeake Bay country on their southward migration from
the Canadian breeding grounds, they usually select a wild rice
marsh or some other fresh tidal river marsh as a feeding
ground (Figure 42). At that time, in the last half of August, the
bluewings have probably been joined by thousands of red-winged
blackbirds, bobolinks or reedbirds, and soras, all attracted to the
largess of the richest marsh community in the Chesapeake Bay
area. A month later, the first Canada geese are drifting into the
lower Chester or Wye rivers where they will be close to a newly
harvested corn field; and by late October, flights of canvasbacks will
be returning to one of last winter's feeding grounds, perhaps a mile
or so south of the mouth of the Patapsco in a slightly brackish
section of the Bay where they can dive for small Baltic clams, now
one of their most important foods. Other waterfowl moving down
the flyway will seek out their special area, some one of a dozen or
more habitats in the Chesapeake Bay country.

Figure 42. Lush mixture of plants in a fresh tidal river marsh along a tributary creek of Patuxent River, Anne Arundel County, Maryland. Wild rice, smartweeds, Walter's millet, arrowhead, arrow arum, and pickerelweed are principal plant species. Prime late summer (late August) habitat of blue-winged and green-winged teals, wood ducks, sora rails, bobolinks, and red-winged blackbirds. Photograph: Brooke Meanley.

Figure 43. Canvasbacks, whistling swans, and a wigeon. More canvasbacks and whistling swans winter in the Chesapeake Bay country than in any other single locality of their wintering range. Photograph: Luther Goldman.

Waterfowl of the Chesapeake Bay Country

Twenty or more years ago, most of the canvasbacks, many geese, swans, dabblers, and some other divers (Figure 43) coming off the fall flight stopped off in the shallows of the estuaries of the upper Bay northeast of Baltimore to feed in the great beds of submerged aquatic vegetation.

Vast beds of submerged plants also occupied extensive areas of the upper Potomac near the District of Columbia, as well as the upper reaches of some of the other tidewater streams. Now we have only small patches scattered about, and mostly in brackish waters. At one time underwater plants, "seaweeds," were the most important foods of most waterfowl, and are still sought after by ducks, geese, and swans.

There are at least twenty species of submerged aquatic plants in Chesapeake Bay. About ten have been predominant, and about seven have been regularly utilized by waterfowl. Those species are wild celery (Figure 44), naiad, muskgrass, redhead-grass, sago pondweed, widgeon grass, and eelgrass (see Appendix for scientific names of plants.

The distribution of submerged plants is correlated with salinities and other physiographic conditions of the Bay (14,15). It thus follows that those species that occur mainly in fresh water are found at the head of the Bay and upstream in the tidal tributaries, and those with high salt tolerances, in the lower Bay sections. Most species seem to occur in moderately brackish zones; virtually all occur in depths of less than ten feet. The terminal ends of most extend to the surface, and close to the land most of the plants are exposed at low tide.

Wild celery, naiad, and muskgrass occur in fresh to slightly brackish water. In Maryland, extensive beds of wild celery formerly

Figure 44. *Right, above,* Wild celery, a favorite submerged aquatic food plant of the canvasback and other diving ducks, grows mainly in fresh and slightly brackish tidal waters of Chesapeake Bay. Photograph: G. Michael Haramis, USFWS. Figure 45. *Right, below,* Slightly brackish estuarine bay. Mouth of Port Tobacco River on the lower Potomac. Photograph: Brooke Meanley.

64

65

Figure 46. Waterfowl biologist Robert E. Stewart of the U.S. Fish and Wildlife Service sampling submerged aquatic vegetation at the Susquehanna Flats in the 1950s. Photograph: Paul F. Springer, USFWS.

extended down along the shallower parts of the Bay from the Susquehanna Flats to about the Patapsco River; and along the Potomac from the District of Columbia to Nanjemoy Creek and Port Tobacco River (Figure 45 & 46) in Charles County. Some areas where wild celery still occurs are in tidal creeks near Baltimore, the upper tidal Patuxent River, Savannah Lake at Elliott Island, and near the mouth of the Port Tobacco. Naiad and muskgrass are found from near the head of the Bay to about the Chester River and in various brackish marsh ponds in the Chesapeake Bay country.

The pondweeds (Figure 47) are the submerged aquatic plants most widely used by diving ducks in North America. The most important species in the Chesapeake Bay country are claspingleaf pondweed or redhead-grass, and sago pondweed (Figure 48). They occur in fresh and brackish water to about twenty-five percent of sea salinity. Both species occurred as secondary submerged aquatics in the Susquehanna Flats area. Today, in the Maryland section of the Bay, redhead-grass is found from about the Patapsco to the Choptank; and sago from the Patapsco to about Tangier Sound.

Widgeon grass has been perhaps the best all-around waterfowl food in the Chesapeake Bay through the years. It is relished by both dabbling ducks and divers. It has a wider tolerance than most other submerged aquatic plants in the Bay, being found mainly from Eastern Bay southward. However, in slightly brackish estuaries, i.e., the Port Tobacco, the Gunpowder, the Middle, and the Patapsco rivers of the upper Bay, widgeon grass reaches its upstream limit where it joins wild celery at its downstream limit. In the 1970s, widgeon grass was fairly abundant in small ponds on Elliott Island and in the nearby Blackwater marshes in Dorchester County and several other areas where it was utilized by black ducks, mallards, wigeons, and gadwalls.

Widgeon grass was named for the waterfowl species the widgeon or baldpate that feeds on it extensively. Ornithologists recently dropped the "d" in the bird's name (it is now wigeon), but the plant's name remains unchanged.

Eelgrass occurs in brackish and salt water, but more in the latter. It grows in normal seawater, and extends upstream in the tidal estuaries to a point where the salt content averages about

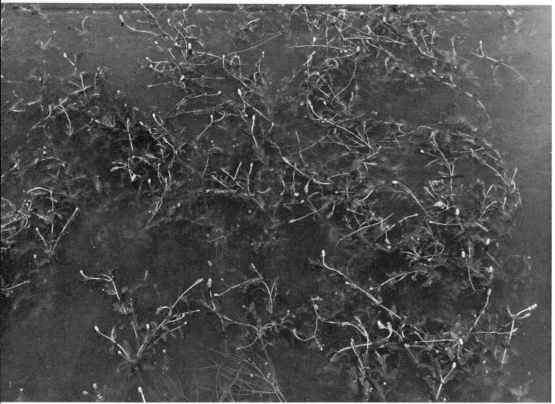

68

Figure 47. *Left, above,* The submerged aquatic plant, slender pondweed (*Potamogeton pusillus*), is found in fresh and slightly brackish waters. Photograph: G. Michael Haramis, USFWS. Figure 48. *Left, below,* Submerged aquatic plants redhead-grass and sago pondweed, *lower left,* prime food of waterfowl, and presently in short supply in the Bay, grow in fresh and brackish tidal waters. Photograph: G. Michael Haramis, USFWS.

Figure 49. *Above,* Fresh estuarine bay marsh, Elliott Island, Dorchester County, Maryland. Photograph: Brooke Meanley.

twenty-five percent of normal sea salinity. It was formerly abundant in coastal bays and sounds where it was a favorite food of the brant. In the Chesapeake it is found from about Eastern Bay southward.

In a recently published report on submerged aquatic vegetation in the Virginia section of the Bay, R.J. Orth et al (16) state that:

> The greatest concentrations of SAV [submerged aquatic vegetation] were found at the mouths of the largest tidal rivers and creeks along the Chesapeake Bay shoreline, and to the east of Tangier and Great Fox islands. Freshwater and low salinity portions of Virginia's tidal rivers were generally found lacking in large areas of SAV . . . .
>
> Based on the co-occurrence of the twenty species found at ninety-three locations throughout Virginia's tidal waters three species associations of SAV were identified. *Zostera marina* [eelgrass] and *Ruppia maritima* [widgeon grass] dominated the higher salinity regions, *Zannichellia palustris* [horned pondweed] and others, the lower salinities region and *Ceratophyllum demersum* [coontail] and others in the freshwater regions. Of the total twenty species of SAV that were identified, eighteen of the species occur primarily within the tidal waters. Species richness was inversely related to salinity with the low salinity areas having the greatest number of species.

Probably no aquatic plant during the last fifty years suffered such a dramatic decline in the Atlantic Coastal region as eelgrass. Its decline was attributed to a protozoan parasite (*Labyrinthula*). Prior to its almost total disappearance in the early 1930s, eelgrass comprised about eighty percent of the brant's food. Since that time it has made somewhat of a comeback, but brant have had to depend more on various forms of algae for food, particularly sea lettuce.

The lush growths of submerged aquatic plants that formerly occurred in the Susquehanna Flats, upper Potomac estuary, and other estuaries of the Bay have largely disappeared because of pollution, turbidity, local changes in salinities, and an exotic competing plant known as Eurasian water milfoil.

Soil erosion in the upper watersheds, and the scouring effect of recent storms such as Hurricane Agnes, have increased turbidity in shallow sections of many of the estuaries. The resulting darkened

Figure 50. Dotted smartweed, *center right foreground*, arrowhead, *lower left*, and wild rice (*taller plants in background*), food plants of dabbling ducks in fresh tidal river marsh. Photograph: Brooke Meanley.

Waterfowl of the Chesapeake Bay Country

waters do not allow for the production of submerged aquatic plants. It is like taking plants from one's sunporch or garden and putting them in the basement or cellar. Hurricane Agnes and other similar storms have carried fresh water into brackish areas of the Bay, thus changing the environment for plants that live in a narrow zone of slight salinities.

Conversely, recent droughts resulted in intrusions of salt water into the upper reaches of fresh tidal sections of rivers thus upsetting the delicate balance of environmental conditions in parts of the estuary where certain plants would exist under normal conditions.

When the exotic Eurasian water milfoil appeared in the Susquehanna Flats about 1958, it crowded out some of the native species. The milfoil began dying out in 1962. Milfoil was not an important food plant of waterfowl. Where sections of the Bay that became polluted or turbid have "freshened up" in recent times, submerged aquatic vegetation is becoming established again.

By the 1970s, with the continued decline of submerged aquatic plants, canvasbacks and some other divers were feeding mainly on two species of clams, *Macoma balthica* and *Rangia cuneata*. *Rangia*, a rather recent invader of the Bay, occurs in brackish water with a salinity of less than fifteen percent of sea strength; whereas *Macoma* is found in water with a salinity of about fifteen to thirty-five percent of sea strength. *Rangia* also occurs in water high in organic matter from sewage discharge. This may be one of the reasons that canvasbacks occur in good numbers at times in Baltimore Harbor. The recent discovery of an exotic small clam known as *Corbicula*, a fresh water shellfish found in the Susquehanna Flats, in the upper James River just south of Richmond, and in the upper tidal Potomac, may add to the variety of waterfowl foods.

Emergent aquatic plants, those that form the marshes, continue to thrive in areas where man is not chipping away at them to develop resorts, and where there has not been excessive siltation or subsidence.

The marsh habitat is important to dabbling ducks and geese. Although Canada geese, black ducks, mallards, pintails, and some of the other dabblers feed on submerged aquatic vegetation and

72

crop residues in agricultural fields, the rootstocks, seeds, and vegetative parts of marsh plants form an important part of the diet of these waterfowl in most parts of their range.

Marshes of the Chesapeake Bay system are mostly of two types: (a) the bay marshes (Figure 49), formed on broad estuarine flats near the Chesapeake itself, Fishing Bay, and other such large embayments; and (b) the river marshes (Figure 50) that occur mainly along the major meander sections of a river, where silt is deposited and forms a substrate for plants.

The plant composition of tidal marshes varies with the location of the marsh, salinities, tides, and yet other factors. The fresh tidal river marshes generally have the richest mixture of flora and are the most productive; but plant species of some brackish marshes may be just as attractive to certain waterfowl. The salt tidal marshes, which usually have fewer species of plants, are less useful to waterfowl in the Chesapeake region. However, along the Delmarva Coast where greater snow geese occur in the greatest numbers, salt-marsh plants such as the cordgrasses may form an important part of their diet.

The most luxuriant fresh tidal river marshes are composed of such waterfowl food plants as wild rice, dotted smartweed, halberd-leaf tearthumb, millet, tidemarsh water hemp, river bulrush, common three-square, rice cut-grass, arrow arum, and arrowhead. In the fresh tidal river marshes, the seeds are the part of the plants relished by most waterfowl. The height of seed production is in late August and early September, timed with the arrival of blue-winged and green-winged teals, wood ducks, and early flights of mallards, black ducks, and pintails. Some food is available in these marshes throughout the fall and winter. Among the finest wild rice marshes of the Chesapeake Bay system are those that are found along the Patuxent River near Upper Marlboro, Maryland, the Elk River at the head of Chesapeake Bay, Mattawoman Creek, a tributary of the Potomac, the Mattaponi and the Pamunkey rivers above West Point, Virginia, and the Chickahominy, a tributary of the James River near Jamestown.

Some plants that occur in the fresh tidal river marshes are also found in the upper reaches of the brackish river marshes. How-

73

Figure 51. Brackish marsh and inlet along Blackwater River, southern Dorchester County, Maryland. Vegetation mostly narrow leaf cattail, Olney three-square, and salt-meadow cordgrass. Habitat of many species of waterfowl, especially black duck, mallard, gadwall, American wigeon, and Canada goose. Photograph: Brooke Meanley.

Figure 52. Winter abode of waterfowl in Patuxent River floodplain forest between Laurel and Bowie, Maryland. On January 31, 1981, Mike Haramis and I saw five female hooded mergansers, eight black ducks, six wood ducks, and three mallards feeding together in the pool, *lower left*. Photograph: Brooke Meanley.

ever, the dominant plant in some brackish rivers in the Chesapeake Bay country is big cordgrass, a tall plant that grows to a height of seven feet or so. Big cordgrass is a good cover plant but has virtually no food value for waterfowl.

The extensive fresh and brackish bay marshes (Figure 51) are important to dabbling ducks, Canada geese, hooded mergansers, and coots. The brackish bay marsh is pocked with numerous ponds that contain submerged aquatic plants, tiny shellfish, snails, and minnows. Olney three-square is a dominant plant in some fresh and brackish bay marshes and is an important food plant of geese in the Blackwater-Elliott Island marshes. Olney three-square is also a component of some brackish river marshes but reaches its best expression in the bay marshes.

Salt-marsh meadows cover expansive areas of brackish and salt bay marshes. The two plants most commonly associated with this community are salt-meadow cordgrass and salt grass. They grow to a height of a foot or less and are of minor value to wintering waterfowl; but the many potholes or ponds in the salt meadow are important feeding places; and during the nesting season, black ducks, blue-winged teals, and gadwalls nest in the meadows.

Salt bay marshes in the Chesapeake Bay area are rather sterile as food producers. Black ducks and occasionally other ducks occur in the tidal creeks that wind through the salt bay marshes. Salt-marsh cordgrass and needlerush are important plants of this marsh type, along with salt-marsh meadows.

Over a period of many years, the character of a marsh may change as it goes through various stages of plant succession. On the Patuxent River marsh near Upper Marlboro, Maryland, a section of wild rice marsh that I worked in thirty years ago is now a shrub swamp, with alders as the predominant plant. Along with the bordering marsh, the shrub swamp is flooded by the tides. Some marsh plants like dotted smartweed grow among the alders in the more open areas, thus attracting various dabbling ducks, particularly blacks and mallards.

Still in the Coastal Plain, but upriver from the tidal marshes, there is often a bottomland or floodplain forest (Figure 52) where wood ducks, blacks, mallards, green-winged teals, and occasionally

76

Figure 53. Aerial photograph of greater snow geese on pond near Berlin, Maryland. Photograph: Jim Goldsberry, USFWS.

blue-winged teals may be found during certain times of the year, particularly during the migration period. This is an important habitat for wood ducks during the nesting season.

Several species of submerged aquatic plants, fish, and crustaceans occur in the bottomland streams; and acorn, beech mast, and seeds of some other forest trees may be a part of a duck's fare in this habitat. A part of the bottomland or floodplain system may be a swamp with standing water most of the year. Such swamps occur along the Pocomoke River in Worcester County, Maryland, near the coast.

The managed habitat, the wildlife refuge, plays a vital role in the well-being of waterfowl on the wintering grounds. Refuges are a complex of varied habitats within a single boundary. Most of them have native marshlands, plant row crops and grasses on the upland part of the area, and have constructed freshwater impoundments, some of which are sown to millets and other aquatics during the drawdown and then flooded in the fall when the waterfowl return. Refuges are the best places to see conveniently a variety of waterfowl.

5

Waterfowl Populations

nnual breeding ground surveys and midwinter inventories conducted by the U.S. Fish and Wildlife Service with cooperating provincial, state, and private conservation agencies, provide an estimate of the number of ducks, geese, and swans in North America. The breeding ground surveys cover an area extending from the Dakotas into Alaska, and are made in May and June with air and ground crews.

The midwinter inventory, made in early January, is an aerial census that measures waterfowl populations in the four flyways, including segments such as Chesapeake Bay. The January inventory is especially adapted to species that congregate in large numbers, particularly the geese (Figure 53) and swans, and several species of diving ducks such as the canvasback (Figure 55) and the scaups. Waterfowl that are scattered through the marshes, the surface-feeding ducks or dabblers, are more difficult to estimate. Many dabblers, however, occur along open waterways, the rivers

Figure 54. Ornithologist Luther Goldman standing behind a duck blind in the Patuxent River marsh counting waterfowl. Photograph: Brooke Meanley.

and larger tidal creeks, and are thus easy to find and count. (See Appendix 1.)

While the midwinter inventory is best for a wide or general coverage of an area such as Chesapeake Bay and other large embayments and coastal sections, the Audubon Christmas Count, conducted by ornithologists (Figure 54) year after year in some of the best areas of waterfowl concentrations, is a valuable adjunct in the effort to monitor local populations. The Christmas Counts, however, are limited in coverage and are by no means a method of estimating total populations in the Chesapeake Bay system.

Christmas Counts are conducted on one day each year, usually between December 15 and January 2, and at the same location. The census or count area is a circle having a diameter of fifteen miles. Usually, somewhere between a dozen and fifty persons participate. Most counts are made in selected areas, those that show the most promise for a variety and abundance of birds.

The prime Christmas Count areas for waterfowl in the Chesapeake Bay country are located in lower Kent County near the mouth of the Chester River; the St. Michaels area on the Miles River; Point Lookout at the mouth of the Potomac; Annapolis-Gibson Island along the western shore; southern Dorchester County in the marshes bordering Fishing Bay, and including Blackwater Refuge; Hopewell on the upper James River just south of Richmond; Newport News near the mouth of the James; and Cape Charles at the mouth of Chesapeake Bay. A few of the Christmas Counts in the Bay area date back to the early 1900s. The counts have become more significant since the 1950s because of more intensive coverage. (See Appendix 2 for Christmas Count data for a five-year period in the 1970s.)

Important information on waterfowl distribution and abundance dating back to the 1920s is contained in *Birds of Maryland and the District of Columbia* (17) by Stewart and Robbins, published in 1958. Dr. H.C. Oberholser of the U.S. Biological Survey was one of the ornithologists that made such estimates of ducks along the Potomac River in the late 1920s. Prior to that time, there was an occasional hunter with an ornithological bent who would make a conscientious effort to estimate the size of large concentrations of

Waterfowl of the Chesapeake Bay Country

waterfowl. Percy T. Blogg and Talbot Denmead, Baltimore hunter-naturalists, were among several that were active in the Chesapeake Bay region in the first quarter of the twentieth century.

Because of its former great abundance, and as the most sought after of waterfowl by hunters, canvasback population estimates were frequently made by wildlife officials as early as the late 1920s and the 1930s. Prior to that time estimates of canvasbacks killed by market hunters were sometimes documented, but total population estimates for the Susquehanna Flats and other important concentration areas were seldom made. Often the hunter and naturalist of earlier times referred to the great numbers of canvasbacks in terms of "clouds of birds" or the "thundering noise" as the birds arose from their resting place.

In reference to canvasbacks on the Flats in the 1930s, H. Albert Hochbaum in his *Travels and Traditions of Waterfowl* (18), states that "crossing the Susquehanna at Havre de Grace was always the highlight of my ride from college at Christmas holidays. Usually some Canvasbacks were in sight of the bridge, and once they were strewn down the river as far as I could see."

What seems to be one of the most notable records of a large concentration of canvasbacks in an area near the Chesapeake Bay was the report of three million birds at Back Bay, Virginia in the early 1900s. This observation was made by Swepson Earle, Conservation Commissioner of Maryland from 1924-35 in his *The Chesapeake Bay Country* (1923) (19). While this figure may be a bit inflated, as are some estimates of extremely large concentrations of birds, those of us who knew Mr. Earle thought of him as an authority on waterfowl.

On November 24, 1934, T. Gilbert Pearson, President of the National Audubon Society, estimated the number of canvasbacks on the Susquehanna Flats at two hundred and fifty thousand (20). And, in November 1937, officials of the Maryland Game and Inland Fish Commission reported an estimated five hundred thousand canvasbacks in the Poole's Island area (21), which is located in the upper Chesapeake Bay near the mouth of the Gunpowder River, and about eight miles down the Bay from the Flats. This figure approximates that of the present (1980) continental popula-

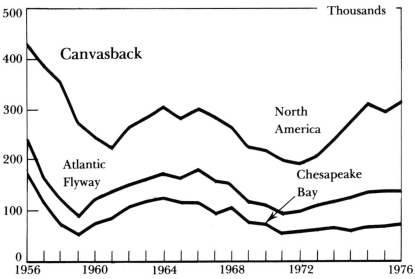

Figure 55. *Above,* Raft of canvasbacks in Chesapeake Bay near Annapolis. Photograph: G. Michael Haramis, USFWS. Figure 56. *Below,* Three-year running average populations of canvasback. From Matthew C. Perry, USFWS.

83

tion. On December 7, 1947, Robert E. Stewart counted more than one hundred thousand canvasbacks and twenty-five thousand scaups from three observation points at the Flats. The last large concentration of canvasbacks reported on the Susquehanna Flats was in the winter of 1952 when 91,000 were seen on the December 27 Christmas Count.

POPULATION TRENDS

In 1979, the size of the continental waterfowl population during the breeding season, based on breeding ground surveys, was estimated at about fifty million birds (see Appendix 3). The estimate for the fall flight after production would be about double the size of the breeding population or approximately one hundred million waterfowl. This also was the approximate size of the continental waterfowl population twenty years ago (1959).

In the decade of the 1950s, the winter population in the Maryland section of the Bay averaged about one million waterfowl; twenty years later, in the decade of the 1970s, the winter population averaged about seven hundred fifty thousand (see Appendix 4). The major changes are in the reduction of populations of most species of ducks (Figure 56-62) and the marked increase in the Canada goose population. The bufflehead is the only duck in Chesapeake Bay that has shown a significant increase in the last twenty-five years (22).

Although the black duck and canvasback winter in greater numbers in the Chesapeake Bay country than in any other section of their range, populations of both species have declined dramatically in the area in the last twenty to twenty-five years. Populations of black ducks are down from about one hundred thirty thousand to fifty thousand and canvasbacks from one hundred ninety-five thousand to sixty thousand.

The continental population of canvasbacks is lower than that of virtually all other widely hunted ducks. Populations of most other species of North American game ducks, except the redhead, are over a million birds.

84

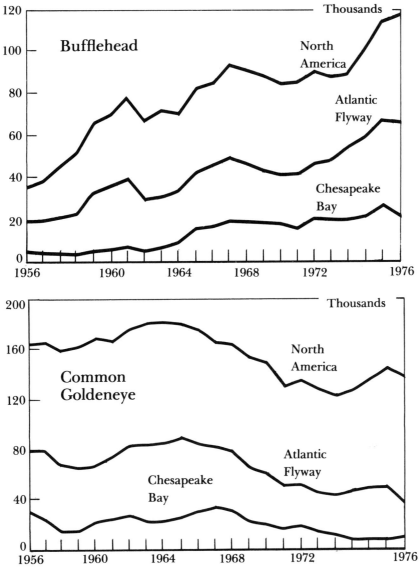

Figure 57. *Above,* Three-year running average populations of bufflehead. From Matthew C. Perry, USFWS. Figure 58. *Below,* Three-year running average populations of common goldeneye. From Matthew C. Perry, USFWS.

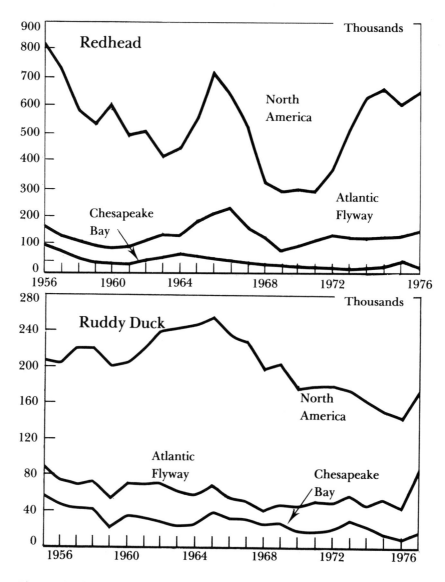

Figure 59. *Above,* Three-year running average populations of redhead. From Matthew C. Perry, USFWS.

Figure 60. *Below,* Three-year running average populations of ruddy duck. From Matthew C. Perry, USFWS.

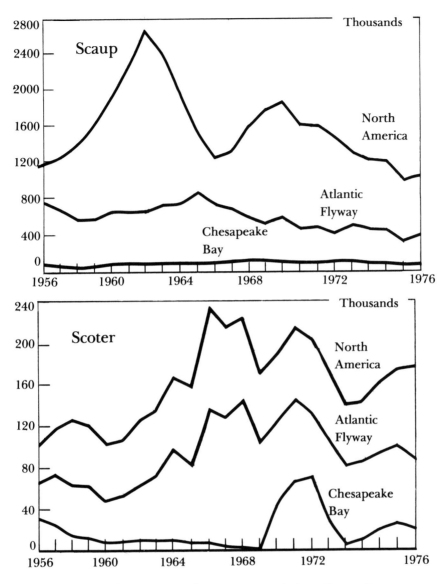

Figure 61. *Above,* Three-year running average populations of scaup. From Matthew C. Perry, USFWS.

Figure 62. *Below,* Three-year running average populations of scoter. From Matthew C. Perry, USFWS.

Waterfowl of the Chesapeake Bay Country

The Canada goose is the most abundant waterfowl species in Chesapeake Bay today. More than one fourth of the continental population winters there. The least abundant during the winter of 1979 were the green-winged teal, blue-winged teal, ring-necked duck, wood duck, and redhead. These species mostly winter south of Chesapeake Bay and, except for the redhead, are much more abundant during migration. The five most widely distributed wintering waterfowl species in over five hundred locations sampled in Tidewater Maryland and Virginia in 1979, were the bufflehead, black duck, mallard, canvasback, and common goldeneye.

In addition to a decline in the number of canvasbacks on the Bay in the last twenty-five years, there has also been a shift in populations from predominance on the Eastern Shore side to the Western Shore. In the period 1953-58, when biologist Robert E. Stewart was conducting his waterfowl surveys in the Maryland section of the Bay, approximately sixty-five percent of the canvasbacks wintered in waters along the Eastern Shore. In the winter of 1979, approximately sixty percent of the canvasbacks wintered on the west side of the Bay (Table 1). The change may have been due to the greater abundance of small clams on the west side. Another factor may be the increase in shoreline feeding of corn to waterfowl by bird lovers on the Western Shore (Figure 63). Canvasbacks and whistling swans are especially attracted to such artificial feeding. The feeding of ducks and swans occurs in many residential sections of the Bay, particularly in the Annapolis-Gibson Island section and the South River-Rhode River area.

LOCAL DISTRIBUTION

The Baltimore Area

Since the Susquehanna Flats are no longer a prime area for waterfowl due to the disappearance of submerged aquatic vegetation, and because there are very few small clams in such fresh estuarine embayments, the Baltimore area is now pretty much the northern limit of appreciable numbers of waterfowl in Chesapeake Bay. This is the slightly brackish section of the upper Bay that extends from about the mouth of the Gunpowder River to the Patapsco River and Baltimore Harbor on the Western Shore.

Figure 63. Canvasbacks and a few mallards feeding on corn along shoreline of Chesapeake Bay near Annapolis. Photograph: G. Michael Haramis, USFWS.

Waterfowl of the Chesapeake Bay Country

Strange as it may seem, Baltimore Harbor, an expanded section of the lower Patapsco River, is a good place for waterfowl. I have seen almost every species of waterfowl inhabiting the Chesapeake Bay region in the harbor, and sometimes numbering in the thousands.

On the December 31, 1979 Christmas Count in the harbor, the following species and their numbers were reported by Robert Ringler, et al:

ruddy duck	2,071	bufflehead	75
canvasback	1,397	American wigeon	44
mallard	1,165	red-breasted merganser	32
lesser scaup	706	whistling swan	18
oldsquaw	209	greater scaup	8
common goldeneye	134	redhead	7
black duck	118	gadwall	1
Canada goose	103	northern shoveler	1
common merganser	86	ring-necked duck	1

TABLE 1

Distribution of Canvasback Populations
in Maryland Section of Chesapeake Bay, 1955-58 and 1979*

1955-58		1979	
Eastern Bay	20%	Patuxent River	24%
Lower Potomac	13	Central Western Shore	20
Choptank River	12	Lower Potomac	12
Chester River	12	Chester River	11
Blackwater-Nanticoke	11	Choptank River	9
Central Western Shore	7	Lower Eastern Shore	7
Patuxent River	7	Blackwater-Nanticoke	3
Coastal Section	5	Upper Western Shore	3
Upper Eastern Shore	5	Upper Eastern Shore	3
Upper Western Shore	3	Coastal Section	3
Lower Eastern Shore	2	Upper Potomac	3
Susquehanna Flats	2	Eastern Bay	2
Upper Potomac	1	Susquehanna Flats	0

*data from U.S. Fish and Wildlife Service

90

Ruddy ducks, canvasbacks, and scoters are among the most frequent visitors to the harbor. Some of the canvasbacks swim around the famous Revolutionary war frigate, the *Constellation*, now permanently docked next to Pratt Street near the heart of the downtown business district. During late December and in January, in the 1970s, as many as 2,000 canvasbacks frequently fed in the outer harbor section off Sparrows Point, near the location of the Bethlehem Steel works.

In this so-called polluted environment, ruddy ducks feed on sludge worms and midge larvae associated with sewage effluent; and canvasbacks are finding some *Rangia* clams and mud crabs. A question of interest, will waterfowl use of the harbor increase if tighter restrictions decrease pollution? There are now more blue crabs in summer, menhaden are showing up, and there are reports of a few bluefish being caught off the piers, suggesting that the harbor is "freshing up."

The Annapolis Area

A lot of waterfowl are concentrated in the Annapolis area because of the five rivers, the Magothy, Severn, South, West, and Rhode that enter the Bay nearby; and the brackish shoal waters of the Bay, optimum for certain molluscan fauna favored by a number of species of diving ducks.

Year after year the Annapolis area is one of the best for canvasbacks in the Chesapeake Bay country. The 1979 January Inventory reported 12,000, second highest for the Bay. In mid-winter canvasbacks in the Annapolis area are usually concentrated in greatest numbers near the Bay Bridge (Figure 64). Biologist Matthew C. Perry who participates in the January aerial surveys says that the Chesapeake Bay Bridge area is also one of the best for greater scaups. A total of 5,790 were reported on the 1973 Annapolis-Gibson Island Christmas Count which includes a part of the Bay Bridge area (see Appendix for Christmas Counts in this area). In mid-January 1981, when most of the upper Bay was frozen, G. Michael Haramis noted that a section of Herring Bay, some eighteen miles south of Annapolis, was still open, and partly because of a raft there of 30,000 ducks, mostly lesser scaup, and a

Figure 64. Canvasbacks and mallards sleeping in opening in ice near Chesapeake Bay Bridge, winter of 1977. This section just above Annapolis, between Gibson Island and Bay Ridge, has been one of the best areas for canvasbacks in Chesapeake Bay for the last thirty years. Photograph: G. Michael Haramis, USFWS.

few canvasbacks and redheads. Northwest winds also keep some sections of the Western Shore open when the rest of the Bay is frozen.

The Patuxent River

In the lower part of the Patuxent River between Benedict and Solomons, 14,336 canvasbacks were counted during the January 1979 Inventory. This was the largest number for a single Chesapeake Bay locality that winter.

The Patuxent is a good river for all kinds of waterfowl because of the Baltic clam beds in its lower reaches and extensive fresh marshes in the upper tidal zone (Figure 65). During storms on the Bay, many dabblers and divers cross the narrow peninsula that divides the Bay and River and fly to the Patuxent where they are better protected by its bordering marshes and wooded hillsides.

On the afternoon of March 24, 1973, John W. Taylor and I were in a canoe along the fresh tidal section of the river observing the spring migration of waterfowl up the Patuxent River Valley. Our bird list for that afternoon included 2,000 Canada geese, 430 green-winged teals, 150 whistling swan, 60 pintails, 60 black ducks, 44 mallards, 43 blue-winged teals, 5 northern shovelers, 4 common mergansers, and 2 American wigeon. Also counted were 323 common snipe and 225 greater yellowlegs.

The Potomac

The tidal estuary of the Potomac is 120 miles long from the District of Columbia to the point where it enters the Bay. The river is 7 miles wide at the mouth.

Looking at a map of the Potomac from the District of Columbia downstream, one is at once aware of the numerous subestuaries, the creeks, bays, and smaller rivers bearing Indian names: Piscataway, Occoquan, Mattawoman, Chicamuxen, Aquia, Nanjemoy, Wicomico, Currioman, Nomini, Yeocomico, and others. These subestuaries and the great river itself form one of the best areas for waterfowl in the Chesapeake Bay system.

In the old days the upper tidal Potomac from Alexandria to the District was noted for its abundant waterfowl populations. As late as the 1920s, the wild rice marshes of the Anacostia River, a confluent of the Potomac that flows through the city of Washington, attracted many ducks, soras, and reedbirds (bobolinks) in the fall. Earlier, Hunting Creek that empties in the Potomac just below the city of Alexandria, was a ducking marsh of George Washington and other founding fathers. Some wild rice still grows there, but the character of the area has changed and most of the marshes bordering the creek have been filled in. It seems that the most extensive wild rice marshes of the Potomac River system today are along Mattawoman Creek, about twenty miles south of the District of Columbia in Charles County, Maryland.

Dr. Harry C. Oberholser, ornithologist with the U.S. Biological Survey (predecessor of the U.S. Fish and Wildlife Service), informed the author that year after year in the 1920s he saw huge rafts of canvasbacks in the river opposite Mt. Vernon, George Washington's home. On February 13, 1926, Dr. Oberholser estimated the number of canvasbacks on the Prince George's County and Charles County, Maryland side of the Potomac at 105,000 birds.

During the 1970s, ruddy ducks were usually the most abundant wintering waterfowl in the District of Columbia area. Rafts of several thousand were often observed opposite Alexandria, where they fed on sludge worms or midge larvae attracted to the effluent from the Blue Plains sewage treatment plant. On the 1978 District of Columbia Christmas Count, which includes a section of the Potomac River near the city, 1,742 ruddies, 685 mallards, 468 black ducks, 333 common mergansers, 68 green-winged teals, and 17 wood ducks were reported. These should be considered fairly high counts for such species in this apparently most polluted section of the river. The common merganser counts at D.C. and fifteen miles south near Ft. Belvoir at 682 were the highest for that species on all Chesapeake Bay Christmas Counts that year; and 1,016 were counted at Ft. Belvoir in 1979. The upper tidal Potomac has long been one of the best areas for common mergansers in the Chesapeake Bay country. A short distance down the river from Ft. Belvoir, at Brooke, Virginia, the following Christmas Counts of com-

Figure 65. The Patuxent River wild rice marsh above Lyon's Creek, Anne Arundel County, Maryland, in winter. On January 22, 1975, I observed the following on this marsh: 600 mallards, 300 Canada geese, 55 pintails, 50 black ducks, 42 wigeons, 30 whistling swans, and 6 scaup (the scaup in the tidal guts). Along with the waterfowl were 30 common snipe, 40 water pipits, and 15 rusty blackbirds. Compare this photograph with the one taken in late summer in the same area (Figure 42). Photograph: Brooke Meanley.

Figure 66. Canvasbacks in trapping area off Persimmon Point, King George County, Virginia. Note Potomac River Bridge crossing between Morgantown, Maryland and Dahlgren, Virginia. Photograph: G. Michael Haramis, USFWS.

mon mergansers have been made: 2,000 in 1955, 2,000 in 1958, and 2,500 in 1962.

Fewer than fifty canvasbacks are usually recorded on the D.C. Christmas Count, but the Ft. Belvoir count, a short distance below Mt. Vernon, often has about a thousand (1,041 in 1978).

Today, most waterfowl occur along the lower part of the river, from about forty miles below the District at Maryland Point, to the mouth. Maryland Point is where there is a great bend in the river as it swings from a north-south trending direction and flows east to southeastward.

Most canvasbacks usually occur on the Virginia side of the river from about Persimmon Point (Figure 66), just above the U.S. 301 (Morgantown) bridge, downstream to Nomini Creek and Currioman Bay, Coan River, and Yeocomico River. Possibly more canvasbacks are on the Virginia side of the river because of the shoal waters which provide greater food resources. The navigational chart for that section of the river bears the name Bottom Kettle Shoals. Waterfowl biologist G. Michael Haramis also found more wintering waterfowl on the south side of the Rappahannock and York rivers.

The section of the river near Pope's Creek at "Wakefield," George Washington's birthplace in Westmoreland County, Virginia, is one of the best areas for canvasbacks and scaups along the Potomac. In the early 1970s, biologists Jim Kerwin and Matthew C. Perry reported 30,000 canvasbacks and similar numbers of scaups off Westmoreland County. But the 1979 January aerial census of the Potomac reported only 10,000 canvasbacks and 15,000 scaups for the entire river; 4,000 canvasbacks were at the mouth of the Wicomico River on the Maryland side opposite Washington's birthplace.

The Chester River Area

During the period 1954-58 when biologist Robert E. Stewart made his intensive survey of Chesapeake Bay waterfowl populations, he stated that the Chester River section (Figure 67) was the most important waterfowl area in Maryland. The January Inventory during that period indicated an average wintering population

Figure 67. An inlet off the Chester River, Queen Anne's County, Maryland. Wintering habitat of whistling swan, canvasback, wigeon, and other waterfowl. Photograph: Brooke Meanley.

of 200,800 waterfowl. In 1979, the lower Chester River section, which also includes lower Kent County and Kent Island, had the largest waterfowl population in the Chesapeake Bay area—250,800 birds. In the 1955-58 years, Canada geese averaged 24 percent of the wintering waterfowl population; in 1979, about 62 percent.

Geese concentrate, or are "held," in this area mainly because of the extensive areas of corn-stubble fields, two large waterfowl preserves (Eastern Neck National Wildlife Refuge and Remington Farms), brackish water with some submerged aquatic vegetation, and brackish marshes.

Corn is the main stay of the Canada goose. Geese particularly like stubble fields with a farm pond where they can get a drink of fresh water and take a bath close to their bounty. In November 1979 I saw a flock of about five hundred Canada geese in and around a farm pond no more than one hundred fifty feet from the back porch of an occupied farm house. Most of these geese came from the northern Canadian wilderness!

Now that the Susquehanna Flats at the head of the Bay are no longer the great staging area for waterfowl coming off the fall flight into the Chesapeake Bay country, the first stop for many ducks, geese, and swans is Eastern Neck Wildlife Refuge, located at the mouth of the Chester River.

When I visited Eastern Neck November 20, 1979, there were approximately thirty thousand geese, five thousand whistling swans, three thousand canvasbacks, and an assortment of other ducks and some coots. Some of the large flocks of Canadas near the refuge on that date had a sprinkling of snow geese.

A flock of approximately five thousand greater snow geese, apparently slightly off course in early January 1980, was seen by Fish and Wildlife Service pilot James R. Goldsberry in an embayment off the Chester River near Queenstown. Greater snows occur in the Delaware River and Bay. However, they are mainly coastal birds. It is not far from Delaware Bay to Queenstown, but greater snows have not been known to frequent upper Chesapeake Bay. Although they are difficult to distinguish from lesser snows, which do frequent Chesapeake Bay in small numbers, the fact that there were no blue phase birds (a color phase of the lesser snow goose) in

Figure 68. Pocomoke Sound, winter habitat of diving ducks, lies between Somerset County, Maryland and Accomack County, Virginia. Goldeneyes, canvasbacks, redheads, buffleheads, oldsquaws, scaup, and scoters feed on submerged aquatic plants and mollusks in these waters. Photograph: Brooke Meanley.

Figure 69. Canvasbacks on lower Choptank River, Dorchester County, Maryland.
Photograph: G. Michael Haramis, USFWS.

a flock of this size would indicate that the flock at Queenstown was greater snow geese.

The Lower Eastern Shore of Maryland

The Chester River and adjacent agricultural fields of the upper Eastern shore and the complex of extensive salt and brackish bays and marshes of southern Dorchester and Somerset counties of the lower Eastern Shore are the two most important waterfowl areas on the east side of the Chesapeake. Eastern Neck National Wildlife Refuge at the mouth of the Chester River is a rallying point for many waterfowl in the upper Eastern Shore section and the same can be said for Blackwater National Wildlife Refuge in southern Dorchester County, in the lower section.

The salt bays (Figure 68) and marshes of the lower Eastern Shore are especially important to waterfowl during exceptionally cold winters when habitats in the upper Bay freeze over. The winter of 1976-77 was extremely cold and virtually all of the Maryland section of the Chesapeake as far south as Tangier Island was frozen solid for several weeks. During that period a large flock of canvasbacks and whistling swans that were fed corn at the water's edge by people in Cambridge were able to keep open a large water hole adjacent to the shore by continued paddling and the heat from their bodies. Another water hole farther out in the Choptank over a clam bed was also kept open for a few days by the continued presence of a flock of canvasbacks (Figure 69).

Commenting on waterfowl habitats of the lower Eastern Shore of Maryland in the mid-1950s. Robert E. Stewart stated, "The salt-water areas ordinarily do not have the high population densities that are characteristic of other habitats in the section, but they are so extensive that they contain more than three-fourth's of the waterfowl."

During the last twenty-five years an increase in the number of Canada geese and a decrease in redheads has been noted in this area. January inventory data for the lower Choptank River in Stewart's study, 1955-58, indicated an average winter population of 117,100 birds. Canada geese comprised twenty-two percent and redheads fifteen percent. In the 1979 winter inventory, approxi-

Figure 70. Part of a flock of 1,200 snow geese and 80,000 Canada geese at Blackwater National Wildlife Refuge, November 3, 1976. Birds with the white heads and necks and darkish bodies are the blue phase of the snow goose, sometimes referred to as the blue goose. Photograph: Brooke Meanley.

mately 107,900 waterfowl were counted on the lower Choptank, and about seventy-seven percent were Canada geese. There were less than 100 redheads. Twenty-five years ago when sago pondweed was abundant in the lower Choptank, Tar Bay, and Honga River, about fifty percent of the redheads of the Maryland section of the Chesapeake wintered in those areas. With the disappearance of much of the sago and other submerged aquatic plants throughout the Chesapeake, redheads, which depend mostly on plant material for their food, correspondingly decreased in numbers in the Bay. The number of redheads in the Maryland section of Chesapeake Bay in the 1953-58 winter period averaged about 66,000 birds. In the winter of 1979, only about 6,000 were reported.

Prior to the 1930s, the lesser snow goose (white and blue phases) was considered a rare bird or accidental visitor in the Chesapeake Bay country. But as more people became involved in Christmas Counts and as more birders took to the field during the winter half of the year, sightings of a few lesser snow geese were reported every year. A noticeable increase was observed after the early 1960s. Since that time, Blackwater National Wildlife Refuge has been the "headquarters" for most of Maryland's small wintering lesser snow goose population (Figure 70). From one to four thousand birds arrive nearly every autumn, usually in late October or early November.

The principal winter range of the lesser snow goose is in the Louisiana-Texas Gulf Coast region, in the Central Valley of California, and with a smaller segment in the interior of Mexico. In the fall flight the eastern spur splits off at James Bay, just south of Hudson Bay, as the Gulf Coast population moves over to the Mississippi Flyway. The continental population of lesser snow geese in the late 1970s was about one and a half million birds. The entire greater snow goose population, most of which winter along the

Figure 71. *Right,* Mixed flight of waterfowl including mallards, pintails, and wigeons. Snow geese are on the ground. Photograph courtesy of Nebraska Game Commission.

104

106

Middle Atlantic coast, usually numbers between fifty to one hundred thousand.

Because of the location, variety of habitats, and protection afforded waterfowl at the Blackwater National Wildlife Refuge and because of the alertness of refuge personnel and visiting birders, a number of unusual birds are sighted there. Two or three white-fronted geese occasionally are reported; on November 4, 1977, Matthew Kershbaum reported fifteen fulvous whistling ducks; and on September 9, 1979, Harry Armistead saw a Eurasian wigeon.

Tidewater Virginia

Tidewater Virginia is the region that lies east of a line from Washington, D.C. to Richmond, and includes the Potomac (south shore), Rappahannock, York, James, and some smaller tributaries of the Bay. As the boundary between Maryland and Virginia, the Potomac River is, by virture of an unusual treaty formalized between the two states in 1877, the property of Maryland to the low tidemark on the Virginia shore. In the January Inventory, Potomac River populations are included in the Maryland report.

The waterfowl population structure of Tidewater Virginia differs little from that of the Maryland section of the Bay, except for the greater number of Canada geese and canvasbacks in Maryland, and the trend toward a greater number of dabblers (Figure 71) in the lower part of the Bay. Canada geese and canvasbacks prefer fresh and slightly brackish waters of the upper Bay. Green-winged teals, northern shovelers, ring-necked ducks, and gadwalls, more southern in their winter distribution, are more abundant in

Figure 72. *Left, above,* Tarpley's Point area, Rappahannock River, Virginia. In January 1979, a flock of about five hundred canvasbacks fed in the coves pictured below. Photograph: Brooke Meanley. Figure 73. *Left, below,* Impoundment at Hog Island Wildlife Refuge, along the south shore of the James River opposite Jamestown. Thousands of pintails, green-winged teals, and other dabblers stop off at this impoundment during migration, and some remain for the winter. Photograph: Brooke Meanley.

the lower part of the Bay; as is the red-breasted merganser, that prefers the saltier sections.

In the lower Chesapeake area in the winter of 1979, the January Inventory reported 3,105 northern shovelers and 1,510 gadwalls at Craney Island near Portsmouth, and 2,500 ring-necked ducks at the Chickahominy River reservoir. The 1979 Inventory for Virginia reported 7,475 gadwalls, 3,618 shovelers, 2,582 green-winged teals, and 2,731 ring-necked ducks; and for Maryland, 400 gadwalls, trace shovelers, trace green-winged teals, and 300 ring-necks. In 1980, the totals for these species were also considerably higher in Virginia.

The best areas for most divers in Tidewater Virginia in the winter of 1979 were along the lower Rappahannock River (Figure 72), where 4,569 ruddies, 778 common goldeneyes, 1,688 buffle-heads, and 3,862 canvasbacks were reported; and Mobjack Bay that had 6,627 ruddies, 1,567 buffleheads, 930 scaup, and 974 common goldeneyes.

Hog Island (Figure 73) and Presquile, state and federal wildlife refuges, are important waterfowl concentration areas along the James River. Presquile reported 525 lesser snow geese on the 1979 January Inventory. The refuge often has the largest number of wintering wood ducks in the Chesapeake Bay Country, with 2,000 in December 1965 and 549 in December 1978. Most wood ducks winter farther south.

Back Bay and Chincoteague

Because they are the two most important waterfowl areas in Virginia and also because of their close geographical relationship to Chesapeake Bay, Back Bay and Chincoteague are included in this narrative. More highest counts of waterfowl species have been made at those two areas than at any other stations in the state. (See *Virginia's Birdlife—An Annotated Checklist*, 1979 (47)).

Figure 74. *Left,* Greater snow geese grazing in salt marsh. In winter they occur near the mouth of Chesapeake Bay and elsewhere along the Middle Atlantic Coast. Photograph: Matthew C. Perry, USFWS.

Figure 75. *Above,* Atlantic brant feeding in Chincoteague Bay, Virginia in winter.
Photograph: Brooke Meanley.

Figure 76. *Above*, Brant over Chincoteague Bay. Photograph: Brooke Meanley.

Waterfowl of the Chesapeake Bay Country

Back Bay is located about fifteen miles south of the mouth of Chesapeake Bay, along the Virginia coast. Much of the habitat is fresh water, and the area is a national wildlife refuge. It is one of the most important wintering areas of the greater snow goose (Figure 74).

Important waterfowl areas at Chincoteague are the Chincoteague National Wildlife Refuge, most of which is located across a small creek from Chincoteague Island on the lower part of Assateague Island; and Chincoteague Bay (Figure 75 & 76) and its bordering salt marshes.

Highest counts in Virginia for each of the following species reported in the Chincoteague area are noted below:

Atlantic brant	32,000	(December 29, 1966)
black scoter	16,300	(December 30, 1964)
black duck	13,400	(December 30, 1964)
white-winged scoter	10,000	(March 24, 1951)
green-winged teal	2,900	(December 3, 1955)
blue-winged teal	2,000	(October 1, 1955)
red-breasted merganser	1,500	(March 18, 1953)
hooded merganser	283	(December 28, 1973)

Highest counts in Virginia for each of the following species reported in the Back Bay area are noted below:

American wigeon	78,850	(December 27, 1969)
greater snow goose	65,000	(December 26, 1964)
redhead	64,000	(1952)
Canada goose	50,000	(winter 1950-51)
pintail	20,000	(winter 1941-42)
lesser scaup	20,000	(December 4, 1939)
whistling swan	14,400	(December 31, 1960)
gadwall	12,000	(December 29, 1974)
ring-necked duck	7,000	(January 1, 1962)

112

6

Food Habits

Mollusks, crustaceans, fish, submerged and emergent aquatic vegetation, and corn in the stubble fields comprise the list of the most important food items that attract waterfowl to the Chesapeake Bay Country in winter. The swans, geese, and surface-feeding ducks or dabblers feed on many of the same food items, particularly at certain seasons. In late summer and early autumn when the first ducks from the north arrive in the Chesapeake Bay area, they frequently congregate in fresh tidal river marshes where the richest mixture of emergent aquatic plants occur and are at the peak of seed production. At that time blue-winged and green-winged teals, mallards, pintails, shovelers, and wood ducks feed mostly on seeds of smartweeds, wild rice, and millet (Figure 77). The wood duck varies its diet at times from the others as it also feeds on the seeds of arrow arum (Figure 78), a food not relished by most other waterfowl. Such seeds are very plentiful in the marsh, but contain oxalic acid crystals, apparently the reason they are seldom taken by other ducks.

113

114

In years past, canvasbacks and other divers, wigeons, whistling swans, and Canada geese arriving at the Susquehanna Flats, all fed on the vast beds of wild celery, sago pondweed, and naiad as long as the upper Bay remained unfrozen.

With the highest energy value of any of our cereal grains, corn is one of the most important foods of many waterfowl on the wintering ground, especially for Canada geese and mallards. It is available to those species in the stubble and is also fed to canvasbacks, swans, and some of the other waterfowl along the shoreline in some residential areas. It is taken by most diving ducks when put out as bait illegally near duck blinds. Francis Uhler, waterfowl food habits specialist (Figure 80), recently told me that scaups taken at Bishop's Head in southern Dorchester County had fed on brown sorghum, a disguised bait that had been put in front of duck blinds.

Waterfowl avail themselves of grain whenever possible. Alexander Wilson, the pioneer ornithologist who more than one hundred fifty years ago described the canvasback as a new species in the scientific literature, stated that in 1812 a vessel loaded with wheat was wrecked at the entrance of Great Egg Harbor in New Jersey. The vessel broke up and grain flowed out over the water toward the land, attracting great numbers of canvasbacks (23).

Waterfowl sometimes gorge themselves with grain and native seeds, occasionally causing impaction and their eventual demise. On one occasion I found a dead Canada goose in a soybean stubble whose esophagus was crammed too full of soybeans. Soybeans expand tremendously when they become wet inside the bird's digestive system.

Figure 77. *Above,* The long narrow seeds of wild rice and the roundish seeds of halberdleaf tearthumb are favorite foods of teals, mallards, blacks, and other dabbling ducks that feed in fresh tidal river marshes. Photograph: Brooke Meanley. Figure 78. *Center,* Fleshy seeds (berries) of arrow arum, a food of wood ducks in fresh tidal river marshes. Photograph: Brooke Meanley. Figure 79. *Below,* Baltic macoma clams, natural size; prime food of canvasbacks and some other diving ducks in the Chesapeake Bay. Photograph: Matthew C. Perry, USFWS.

115

Waterfowl of the Chesapeake Bay Country

It is amazing how many thousands of small seeds are often taken in a single meal by one duck or goose. A black duck collected in Dorchester County, Maryland had taken 18,000 seeds of dotted smartweed.

Waterfowl will feed on all parts of some aquatic plants, the seeds, stems, leaves, and roots, but are quite selective with other plants. When wild celery is available, canvasbacks feed mostly on the subterranean roots and winter buds of that submerged aquatic plant, discarding the green leaves. As biologist Matthew C. Perry points out, this practice is common in other diving ducks and demonstrates the ability of ducks to select plants and parts of plants that best meet their nutritional needs. Aquatic plant foods, especially the tubers and rootstocks apparently provide the maximum energy possible during the cold winter months.

Waterfowl, seemingly out of character, sometimes take rather odd food items, indirectly or otherwise. Clarence Cottam reported on several greater scaup stomachs that contained remains of a field mouse, a lemming, and a sponge (24). And a pintail stomach from Dorchester County, Maryland contained the seeds of blackberry and poison ivy.

Food items pass through the digestive tract quite rapidly. John Grandy determined that a blue mussel can pass through the digestive tract of a black duck in thirty to forty minutes (25). Matthew C. Perry force fed mallards the hard-shelled *Rangia* clams and found that they were completely ground up in the gizzard and passed into the intestine in fifteen minutes.

Large rafts of feeding canvasbacks and scaups are often tended by other species of ducks, and by swans and coots. At some of these congregations there is commensalism and parasitism in the feeding process. Forbush and May have described such food piracy by the wigeon or baldpate:

> In southern waters where Canvas-backs, Redheads, and Greater and Lesser Scaups, all excellent divers, are numerous and are diving continually on the feeding grounds, bringing up succulent roots, bulbs, and other parts of submerged water-plants, the active Baldpate waxes fat by stealing tidbits from the hard-working diving ducks. The moment a bird comes to the

116

Figure 80. Francis Uhler, biologist with the U.S. Fish and Wildlife Service, examining the contents of waterfowl stomachs for the purpose of identifying food items and determining their frequency of occurrence and volume. This painstaking microscopic procedure involves the separation of hundreds of ground-up particles. Extensive reference collections of aquatic plants, especially seeds, aquatic insects, mollusks, crustaceans, and fish are necessary as an aid to identification. Photograph: Matthew C. Perry, USFWS.

surface, one or more Baldpates dash in, and sometimes one may succeed in snatching a morsel from the bill of the industrious diver (26).

I have seen whistling swans attended by wigeons, coots, and ring-billed gulls, waiting around for bits of submerged aquatic vegetation to come floating to the surface as the swans tore loose pondweeds and wild celery from the bottom of a shallow embayment.

Pintails, mallards, and some other waterfowl feed during the day and night. During the hunting season, especially when there is heavy shooting in certain areas, waterfowl that normally do much of their feeding in the day may switch to night feeding. The wigeon is well known for this change. The feeding period of some of the divers varies with the tide. They tend to feed closer to shore at high tide.

The Swans

Whistling swans forage in shallow water on submerged aquatic plants and certain mollusks; and on land where they are essentially grazers and grubbers, sometimes pulling up and eating entire plants.

Robert E. Stewart (11) examined the gullet and gizzard contents of fifty whistling swans from Chesapeake Bay during the period 1953-58, and reported the following items:

> Leaves, stems, and roots of submerged plants appear to be the foods of paramount importance to Whistling Swans in all areas where the birds occur in greatest concentrations. Wild celery apparently is the principal food in fresh estuarine bays, whereas widgeon grass and sago pondweed are utilized to the greatest extent in the critical brackish estuarine bay communities. Certain species of thin-shelled bivalve mollusks, particularly the Baltic macoma (*Macoma balthica*) and the commercially valuable long or "soft-shelled" clam (*Mya arenaria*) are also consumed in considerable quantities in the brackish estuarine bays. The small population of swans on the estuarine bay marsh ponds in Dorchester County show their adaptability by consuming not only widgeon grass but other entirely different types of food, including rootstalks and stems of certain emergent marsh plants.

118

In the 1970s there was less feeding on submerged aquatic vegetation, more on small mollusks, and much more feeding in agricultural crop stubble and winter wheat fields.

The Geese

In addition to feeding on corn in stubble fields, grazing in pastures, fallow fields, and on fescue and other grasses planted for them on wildlife refuges, Canada geese also dig up roots of certain plants such as Olney three-square that grow in some fresh and brackish tidal marshes.

Lesser snow geese have much the same food habits as Canada geese, but feed more on native marsh plants. They are mainly grubbers, and in the course of foraging on Olney three-square often do devastating damage to the marshes, clearing out extensive areas so that there is nothing left except the bare substrate of peat or mud.

Greater snow geese, coastal in distribution, feed mainly on salt-marsh plants, uprooting the cordgrasses; but in the Back Bay area of southeastern Virginia I have seen them feeding in fresh marshes on the rhizomes of cattails.

Atlantic brant, also occurring mainly along the coast, with a few in the lower Chesapeake, forage mostly on marine algae and eel-grass. When the salt marsh and salt bays freeze over, they graze on grasses in people's front yards at Chincoteague and other villages along the Middle Atlantic Coast.

The Surface-feeding or Dabbling Ducks

The dabblers feed along the surface of the water scooping up seeds of marsh plants. They may forage with head and neck immersed, and by upending to obtain the top parts of submerged aquatic plants that are near the surface of the water, and for invertebrates on the muddy bottom of the shallows. They rarely dive for food.

Robert E. Stewart (11) reported the gullet and gizzard contents of wild mallards from several different areas and habitats in the Maryland section of the Chesapeake Bay country. Eighty-five birds were examined from collections made in the period 1955-58. In a

Waterfowl of the Chesapeake Bay Country

series of thirteen birds mostly from the Chester River, Eastern Bay, and the Choptank River areas, seeds and leaves of widgeon grass and redhead-grass and kernels of corn were the most important foods. Eleven birds mostly from fresh tidal river marshes of the Patuxent River fed on seeds of dotted smartweed, softstem bulrush, common three-square, halberdleaf tearthumb, and arrow arum. Principal foods of twenty-eight birds taken in brackish bay marshes in the Blackwater-Nanticoke area were seeds, leaves, stems, and rootstalks of widgeon grass, seeds of Olney three-square and twigrush, and kernels of corn. Foods of seventeen mallards collected in the Patuxent River wooded bottomlands between Laurel and Bowie were mainly beech nuts, white oak acorns, seeds of hornbeam, and the vegetative parts of an alga. Aquatic animal life is a minor part of the mallard's diet on the wintering ground.

Biologists Matthew C. Perry and Francis Uhler found seventy-six different food items in a series of mallards taken during the hunting season in the Curle's Neck area along the upper James River near Richmond, Virginia in the fall of 1978. Corn was the major item, as it is today in most of the Chesapeake Bay country (27).

The closely related black duck is found in much the same habitats as the mallard and feeds on much the same foods, but additionally occurs in salt marsh and saltwater habitats seldom visited by mallards. Blacks also feed on a wider variety and greater volume of animal foods, including salt-marsh snails, ribbed mussels, and fish, and in summer, on mosquito larvae and pupae.

In the stomach of a black duck, collected by Robert E. Stewart in southern Dorchester County on December 31, 1948, seeds of salt-marsh cordgrass had formed eighty percent of its diet, indicative of foraging in a salt-marsh habitat. Another black duck taken in the same area on the same date had been feeding mainly in a salt-marsh pond on top minnows (fifty percent), dragonfly nymphs (twenty-three percent), giant waterbugs (eighteen percent), small snails (six percent), and seeds of twigrush (three percent).

The pintail feeds on some of the same foods as the mallard and black duck, but, as pointed out by Palmer in the *Handbook of North*

120

American Birds, "has considerably narrower environmental preferences than the mallard, with which it commonly associates."

During the migration period, pintails sometimes show up in wooded bottoms. One taken in a bottomland forest near Laurel, Maryland by Robert E. Stewart in November had eaten snails and mollusks from the stream and seeds of ironwood, buttonwood, poison ivy, and sweet gum.

The teals are essentially marsh ducks and seed eaters, preferring the small seeds of such aquatic plants as millets, smartweeds, sedges, and widgeon grass. Vegetable foods form seventy percent or more of their diet on the wintering grounds.

Perry and Uhler (27) reported on the foods of twenty-nine green-winged teals that had fed on fifty-six different food items. The speciments were obtained during the hunting season in the mid-1970s in the Curle's Neck area of the James River just east of Richmond. Seventy-three percent of the plant foods were seeds of four species of sedges. Only eight percent of the food was animal matter—dragonfly nymphs and tiny crustaceans.

Like the teals, the wigeon and gadwall are preeminently vegetarians. Plant food items form ninety percent or more of their food during the winter in the Chesapeake Bay country. Their most important foods are submerged aquatic plants, especially those that are found in a brackish environment, the pondweeds, eelgrass, and widgeon grass. They do, however, forage in other estuarine environments, and in a fresh tidal river marsh at Curle's Neck in the 1970s, the starchy rootstocks of rice cut-grass formed fifty percent of the food of five wigeons examined by Perry and Uhler.

Wigeon appear to feed more on soft aquatic vegetation than on seeds. According to Perry, the grit that they use for grinding, reflects their feeding habits, as it is usually fine sand which is used to break down the cells of the vegetation. Gravel is often found in the gizzards of birds that feed on seeds which are harder to grind.

The shoveler, another dabbler, has at times been observed foraging in a manner different from most other ducks. Frank Bellrose, author of *Ducks, Geese, and Swans of North America* (5), described the procedure:

121

Waterfowl of the Chesapeake Bay Country

The shoveler, which feeds actively in both deep and shallow waters, has the most unusual feeding habits of any duck. In deep water it apparently feeds on surface plankton. I have often watched shovelers feeding on the surface of lakes devoid of aquatic vegetation. A steady stream of water is taken in by the tip of the bill and jetted out at the base. From a tower, I have seen clear paths in the wake of their feeding passage through green waters rich in phytoplankton (an aggregate of small floating plant organisms). Occasionally a pair of shovelers rotate their bodies head to head, apparently stirring up the plankton-ladened waters and straining them through the lamellae (comb-like structure) of their bills.

Shovelers occur in a wide variety of habitats in the Chesapeake Bay country, with some of the largest concentrations in refuge impoundments. Individuals and pairs regularly occur in small ponds in the Blackwater-Elliott Island brackish marshes. Principal plant foods in a series of twelve stomachs of birds collected in brackish estuarine bay marshes in southern Dorchester County included seeds of Olney three-square, widgeon grass, salt grass, and the vegetative parts of muskgrass. Important animal foods were small mollusks, crustaceans, and minnows (Stewart).

As its name implies, the wood duck spends much of its time in a woodland environment, viz., along river bottomlands and wooded ponds. The most important foods in river bottomlands or flood-plain forests are beech nuts, acorns of several species of oaks, and fruits and seeds of other woodland plants.

The Diving Ducks

The divers have the large lobe on the hind toe (not present in dabblers) that aids in diving. Most feeding by this group is in relatively shallow depths, averaging from about three to fifteen feet, except perhaps in the sea ducks, the scoters and oldsquaw, which frequently dive to thirty feet or more. There are some extraordinary records of oldsquaws being caught in gill nets at depths of over one hundred feet.

Divers usually remain under water for ten to thirty seconds. Diving for food may continue for long periods. A male bufflehead

122

was observed to make no less than eighty consecutive dives in forty-three minutes. In some species there is synchrony in feeding activities. Palmer (3) reported that a flock of buffleheads are frequently below the surface simultaneously.

Ducks of the genus *Aythya* (the pochards) possess some of the food habits of both the dabblers and the sea ducks. Like the dabblers, the canvasback, redhead, ring-necked duck, and the scaups feed on a high percentage of plant material when it is available, but also utilize shell fish, principal diet of the scoters and oldsquaw.

The canvasback's food habits in Chesapeake Bay have been extensively studied during the past twenty-five years, mostly by biologists of the U.S. Fish and Wildlife Service, Francis M. Uhler, Matthew C. Perry, and Robert E. Stewart. In the 1950s Stewart analyzed the foods of canvasbacks from several different habitats, thus the types of food can be related to salinity and other physiographic conditions. In this series of stomachs, some thirty-three different food items were identified; less than a dozen were of major importance to the canvasback.

In the *fresh estuarine embayments* of the Susquehanna Flats, Sassafras, and Gunpowder rivers important foods in thirty stomachs were leaves, stems, rootstocks of wild celery, and sago pondweed. Also taken were the seeds of sago and claspingleaf pondweeds. The only animal food consumed were larvae of mayflies, a minor item.

In the *brackish estuarine bays* of the Chester River, Eastern Bay, and the Choptank River, the principal foods in forty-one stomachs were various mollusks and crustaceans, particularly the small Baltic clam (Figure 79), and mud crabs. Also taken were leaves, stems, rootstocks and seeds of claspingleaf pondweed, eelgrass, widgeon grass, and bait corn.

Foods of nine canvasbacks from the *brackish* waters of Fishing Bay and the Nanticoke River, and six stomachs from the *salt* waters in lower Dorchester County and adjacent Virginia waters, were mainly Baltic clams and bait corn.

In the 1970s and 1980s Perry and Uhler found the Baltic clam to be the most important food of the canvasback (eighty to ninety percent). The vegetative parts and seeds of wild celery, redhead-grass, and widgeon grass were a minor item in the overall picture. However, where some habitats had freshened up or become less polluted, local growths of submerged aquatic vegetation were present and utilized. Uhler reported canvasbacks and whistling swans feeding in extensive beds of wild celery in Savannah Lake, located at Elliott Island, Dorchester County. In the winter of 1979 G. Michael Haramis found canvasbacks frequently in a small area of the Potomac that extends from about Dahlgren to Maryland Point, where wild celery, redhead-grass, and widgeon grass occurred, and I observed canvasbacks feeding on redhead-grass in a cove along the lower Chester River in November 1979.

Foods of canvasbacks vary locally. Uhler examined several stomachs from the Dahlgren, Virginia section of the Potomac in 1978 that contained mostly scuds, an amphipod crustacean; and Perry and Uhler examined a series of stomachs of birds taken in a sewage lagoon in southern Maryland that contained midge larvae. Midges are small flys.

Clarence Cottam (24) examined 427 canvasback stomachs collected in various localities in North America and made the following interesting notations regarding food items taken: 23 species of plant and animal foods were taken in a single meal; 93 food storage buds were found in a single stomach; and 79 canvasbacks made a meal of only one food item. The average meal, however, was composed of 188 individual items or particles of food of about five to six species of plants and/or animals.

The redhead often associates with the canvasback when feeding, thus their diets are much the same in some areas. But the redhead tends to be more of a vegetarian and in general winters a little farther south in the Bay, where it is uncommon now, as is the vegetation.

Greater and lesser scaups commonly feed with canvasbacks and redheads on the same plant and animal foods; but they also form large rafts of their own and generally have a greater propensity for animal foods, viz., clams, mussels, and crustaceans.

J.M. Cronan (28) made the following interesting observations on the foraging habits of greater scaups in winter in Connecticut: birds fed at any daylight hour and took submerged mussels at all levels of tide. They fed regardless of rain, snow, and sleet, even when there were three-foot waves, and in breaking surf. They fed readily among various ducks. Herring gulls often robbed them of food, but this interferred little with their feeding. Their average time of submergence in feeding dives was 20.4 seconds. The pause between dives was slightly less than the duration of submergence.

The other member of the genus *Aythya*, the ring-necked duck, is more of a freshwater bird, often frequenting lakes and the larger wooded ponds, where it feeds on small acorns, larvae and nymphs of aquatic insects, and seeds of marsh plants that grow around the edges of ponds and lakes. Where the ring-necked ducks occur along tidal rivers, they feed on much the same foods as the canvasback. Most ringnecks pass through the Chesapeake Bay country on migration, wintering in the South.

The common goldeneye and bufflehead, somewhat closely allied on the wintering ground, have much the same food habits. Their foods fall somewhat between the canvasbacks, redheads, and scaups on the one hand and the sea ducks on the other. They winter mostly in extensive brackish and salt bays and the lower reaches of rivers, feeding on mollusks and crustaceans, including barnacles.

The Sea Ducks

The white-winged, surf, and black scoters and the oldsquaw are birds mainly of extensive open water areas, the Bay proper, the coastal embayments such as Chincoteague Bay, and the oceanic littoral zone, where they feed on clams, blue crabs, mud crabs, crayfish, finfish, aquatic insects, and to a lesser extent on aquatic plants. Stewart examined the stomach of one oldsquaw that had taken corn and wheat, no doubt bait from in front of a duck blind, as the sea ducks do not feed on land.

The Ruddy Duck

The ruddy is a widely distributed bird that might show up anywhere in tidal and nontidal waters. It usually occurs in flocks, often sizeable, in slightly brackish areas. As we have reported, for twenty or more years, flocks of several thousand birds spend parts of the winter opposite Alexandria (in the D.C. area) and in Baltimore Harbor feeding on sludge worms and midge larvae. Otherwise, the ruddy more typically occurs in the same habitats as the canvasback, and with somewhat similar food preferences.

The Mergansers

In the Chesapeake Bay country hooded and common mergansers occur mainly in fresh and slightly brackish water; while the red-breasted merganser is more of a saltwater bird, but occasionally occurs in freshwater habitats, especially during the migration periods. The principal diet of mergansers is fish; but the hooded merganser feeds less on fish than the other two mergansers.

Two red-breasted mergansers from the lower Eastern Shore of Maryland in salt bay habitats had fed on johnny darters and common prawns; three from fresh tidal areas of the Potomac River had fed chiefly on sunfish, minnows, and amphipod crustaceans (11).

Red-breasted mergansers frequently form sizeable flocks and coordinate fish hunting by swimming somewhat abreast and driving small fish into shallow water where they are easily caught.

Hooded mergansers forage as singles, in pairs or in small groups. The gullets and gizzards of ten birds taken in various habitats and examined by Robert E. Stewart contained several kinds of small fish and evidence of mud crabs, crayfish, dragonfly nymphs, and caddisfly larvae.

Two common mergansers collected by Stewart in a fresh tidal section of the Potomac, had eaten pumpkinseed sunfish and yellow perch.

7

Marking Techniques
and Population Studies

TRAPPING AND BANDING CANVASBACKS

The banding of waterfowl and other birds is one of the
most valuable tools of wildlife management. Properly
designed, banding studies allow biologists to monitor
the vital signs of a population and estimate the key
parameters necessary to determine population status. Banding
data provide information on the age and sex structure of a population and on the rates of recruitment and survival. Knowledge of
survival rate, particularly of females and young is an important
measure of population well-being.

Among waterfowl, females generally have higher rates of mortality. This is due to higher female losses during nesting and the
brood rearing period. Also, females and particularly young of both
sexes are known to be more vulnerable to hunting than adult males.

Banding is also a valuable aid in determining migration routes
and movements of individual birds. Wildlife refuges or sanctuaries
are established along paths of migration where waterfowl can have a
place to rest and feed, breed, and winter in peaceful surroundings.

127

Figure 81. Diving duck trap and captured canvasbacks. Birds are banded and released. Sex and age ratios are also determined from the trapping operation. Note mallard ducks in foreground. Photograph: Matthew C. Perry, USFWS.

Figure 82. On the Choptank River waterfowl biologist G. Michael Haramis at trap handing male canvasback to biologist Lois Moyer for banding. Photograph: Matthew C. Perry, USFWS.

Waterfowl of the Chesapeake Bay Country

Approximately thirty-five thousand canvasbacks have been banded in the Chesapeake Bay area. Over ten thousand were banded in the 1970s. Most of the recent banding has been done by biologists G. Michael Haramis and Matthew C. Perry and assistants of the Patuxent Wildlife Research Center (Figure 81, 82, & 83).

The principal areas of banding in recent years have been in the Bay off Gibson Island, and nearby Bay Ridge; at Rhode River, located a few miles from Annapolis; Potomac River, mainly off King George and Westmoreland counties, Virginia; near the mouth of the Wicomico where it enters the Potomac; and along the lower Choptank River.

Preliminary to trapping, bait is placed in front of the traps for three or four days before the operation begins, to lure the birds to the area. As the birds are attracted to the trapping area, the traps are then baited and set in the predawn hours. The best time for trapping is at about dawn, which is the most active feeding period. Tides, wind, and ice may affect the trapping operation adversely; on the other hand, threatening stormy weather often stimulates the birds to feed.

As many as five hundred birds are sometimes trapped in a day. Captured birds are weighed, aged and sexed, banded, and released. In addition to canvasbacks, other waterfowl species trapped in order of abundance are lesser scaups, greater scaups, ring-necked ducks, redheads, buffleheads, and common goldeneyes.

A number of recent recoveries of canvasbacks have been made in Saskatchewan and Manitoba, and in Minnesota and Wisconsin. Those taken by hunters, mainly in October and November, in Minnesota and Wisconsin were on a migration path, probably to the Chesapeake Bay and other eastern wintering grounds.

There have been several returns of long-lived birds in the Chesapeake Bay area. A canvasback banded in the summer of 1965

Figure 83. *Right,* Banding a male canvasback at Cove Point, Calvert County, Maryland, winter of 1972. Photograph: Matthew C. Perry, USFWS.

131

Figure 84. Radio telemetry is one of the techniques used to obtain data on the movements and other activities of waterfowl. The transmitters are attached to the duck's bill or back. Photograph: Matthew C. Perry, USFWS.

in North Dakota was recovered at Gibson Island fifteen and one-half years later; and a canvasback banded at Kent Island, Maryland in 1963, was recovered at Kent Island sixteen and one-half years later.

An adjunct to the canvasback banding operation has been a study of local and regional movements by color marking and with radio transmitters attached to the birds. In the fall and winter of 1972-73, Matthew C. Perry and associates dyed 1,449 canvasbacks at several locations in the Bay. Over ninety-five percent of the observations from November 1972 to February 1973 of the dyed birds were from the Chesapeake Bay, indicating that most canvasbacks that arrive at the Bay in November and December do not migrate farther south. There were only two sightings from this sample south of Chesapeake Bay, both in North Carolina. Northward movement, however, was more common in the winter of this study, as nineteen color-marked birds were reported from the North Atlantic States during sometime in December, January, and February. The February birds may have already started their migration toward the breeding grounds.

In the winter of 1973-74, waterfowl biologist Perry color-marked 211 male canvasbacks in Baltimore Harbor with pink dye, and 103 males on the lower Potomac River with blue dye. Although some sightings were reported from different locations of the Bay, most birds had strong attachments to the original marking area and remained there throughout the winter.

One canvasback instrumented with a radio transmitter (Figure 84) at Cove Point in Calvert County, Maryland on January 15 was located at Jamaica Point, Choptank River, Maryland on January 24 and 31 and then off Gibson Island on February 5 and 7.

In the course of banding operations on the lower Choptank River, Biologist G. Michael Haramis observed that canvasbacks have a distinct morning flight which occurs about thirty minutes before sunrise. The morning flight was from the west, indicating that the canvasbacks came from the mouth of the Choptank or beyond in the broader and deeper waters of the Chesapeake. In a matter of fifteen minutes or so, several thousand birds may drop in.

134

Marking Techniques and Population Studies

The evening roost flight down river occurred less synchronized, with only small groups of birds leaving before dark had set in.

Biologist Haramis states that through banding we have observed that groups of canvasbacks tend to come home to specific wintering areas on the Bay, and although some mixing occurs with time, a large percentage of the flock remains intact.

Canvasbacks winter-banded in Chesapeake Bay have been reported all along the migration corridor to the central prairies and Canadian provinces, but few have been reported from other flyways. This indicates the strong traditional wintering tendency of the Bay population.

THE USE OF NECK COLLARS

In the last decade or so, waterfowl biologists have been using numbered neck collars (Figure 85) in the study of local and migratory movements of waterfowl, especially the larger species. Dr. William J.L. Sladen and associates of Johns Hopkins University have been using this technique for charting the movements of whistling swans to and from Chesapeake Bay wintering grounds and arctic breeding grounds, using an internationally coordinated marking system. The color-coded neck bands identify an individual bird from 300 yards with a spotting scope.

Between January and March 1970, Dr. Sladen and colleagues marked 300 whistling swans with numbered neck collars in Maryland. In the following winter, 1970-71, over half of the marked birds were resighted back in Maryland, Virginia, or North Carolina, after a migration to and from the arctic.

Of forty-eight swans marked with numbered neck collars in the Rhode River-West River area near Annapolis, forty-four

Figure 85. *Left*, Numbered neck collar placed on Canada goose for use in studies of local movements and migration. The number on the collar is large enough to be seen at several hundred yards with a spotting scope. Photograph: Matthew C. Perry, USFWS.

135

(ninety-two percent) were individually identified during the first year after banding. Two of the birds were resighted on their breeding grounds on the Northern Slope of Alaska. Of ten birds marked with neck collars near Prudhoe Bay on the Northern Slope in August 1971, eight were resighted the following winter in Maryland, Virginia, and North Carolina (29).

8

The Bald Eagle and Waterfowl

There seems to be a correlation between the distribution of waterfowl and bald eagle populations in the Chesapeake Bay Country. Two of the best areas for waterfowl in the Bay area are the Blackwater section in Dorchester County, Maryland and the Potomac River, from about Pope's Creek to Potomac Creek on the Virginia shore. In the 1970s these two areas usually had the highest density of bald eagles. Forty were seen on the December 26, 1979 Christmas Count in the Blackwater area.

Prior to the 1950s, the Susquehanna Flats and the upper Chesapeake section were one of the most important waterfowl concentration areas in the Bay. During the years 1935-37, I visited eleven active bald eagle nests in the upper Chesapeake region; there were probably several nests that I did not know about. There were four nests on the Edgewood Arsenal peninsula that lies between the Bush and Gunpowder rivers; three on the Aberdeen Proving Grounds, which borders the Flats; one on Spesutie Island

Waterfowl of the Chesapeake Bay Country

(Figure 86), which lies just off the Proving Grounds, out in the Flats; one near Chesapeake City, one on the west side of the Gunpowder estuary; and one in the Carroll's Island section, closer to Baltimore. Today (1980), the upper Chesapeake section is no longer a prime area for wintering waterfowl *or* nesting bald eagles.

Predatory birds are usually associated with dense populations of certain prey species. I observed such predator-prey relationships when investigating large blackbird roosts. At or in sight of a roost of an estimated twenty million blackbirds in a fourteen-acre thicket near Stuttgart, Arkansas on the late afternoon of January 20, 1953, seventy-nine predatory birds were observed, including seventy-four hawks of three species and five owls of three species.

Eagles depend on waterfowl for food to some extent in the winter and fish and other birds during most of the rest of the year.

Frank Smith, a biologist at the Blackwater National Wildlife Refuge in the 1930s, examined 59 regurgitated bald eagle pellets from that area (30). He found that birds, mostly waterfowl, constituted 50.4 percent of the food items. Among waterfowl identified were Atlantic brant, mallard, pintail, green-winged teal, wigeon, wood duck, and canvasbacks. Fish formed only 4.2 percent. But in a sample of food remains taken at several Chesapeake Bay eagle nests in 1936 and 1937 by Bruce Overington and W. Bryant Tyrrell, fish comprised 52.4 percent of all food taken. Bird remains, mostly water birds, formed 33.3 percent (31). Being familiar with the field work of Smith and of Overington and Tyrrell, I recall that the latter two ornithologists examined nests later in the spring.

Much of the eagle's food is carrion—carrion being dead animals that would include fish, waterfowl, muskrats, and other creatures of the Bay and its marshes. Probably most waterfowl taken by eagles are birds that have been wounded by hunters and are unable to fly, or if so, only feebly.

In his *Life Histories of North American Birds of Prey*, part 1 (32) A.C. Bent states:

> In certain places, particularly in winter, bald eagles live largely
> on waterfowl, mainly geese, brant, ducks, and coots. The eagle
> is perfectly capable of catching a duck on the wing and fre-
> quently does so; but oftener the duck is pounced upon in the

138

Figure 86. A huge nest of the bald eagle on Spesutie Island, Susquehanna Flats, February 1936. This nest was 115 feet from the ground, approximately 7 feet deep and 6 feet across at the top. There were at least a half dozen active eagle nests in the vicinity of the Flats during the 1930s. There were also a half million waterfowl, mostly canvasbacks, concentrated in the area in the late fall and early winter. Photograph: Brooke Meanley.

water or forced to dive again and again until it becomes exhausted and is easily captured; frequently two eagles join in the chase, which gives the poor victim a slim chance to escape. I have seen two eagles chasing a black duck in the air until it was forced down into the water. Ducks killed by sportsmen are often picked up by eagles. In Florida, coots (*Fulica*) are very abundant in winter and furnish a favorite food supply for the eagles. Dr. W.L. Ralph (Bendire, 1892) says that many are caught on the wing; he found the remains of 13 in one nest.

The coot is a member of the rail family that in general conformation resembles a duck, and associates with waterfowl.

Gilbert Klingel in his *The Bay* (33) recounts the interesting episode of an eagle capturing a duck on the Potomac River.

In full action an eagle is a never-to-be-forgotten sight. I remember a fall day on the Potomac several years ago. It was one of those times when innumerable flocks of ducks were moving about, skimming in groups a few feet above the water. One such flight, of about thirty individuals, was moving down river when suddenly every duck, as one bird, veered and then plummeted to the surface of the water. They landed with a simultaneous splash and then scattered in all directions. And not a moment too soon, for out of the seemingly empty sky came hurtling the form of a full-grown eagle. The big bird was plunging from the heights like an arrow, white head and tail flashing in the sun. It had been aiming at the center of the group and the sudden dispersal of its selected prey temporarily disconcerted it, for it quickly veered skyward again, mounted to a hundred feet or so, and then with broad beating wings took off after one of the fowl which by this time had burst into flight again and was fleeing for safety as fast as it could go. But the duck did not have a chance; with ease the eagle overtook its quarry and then once again plunged. The duck and the eagle hit the water together—a mass of flying spray and vibrating feathers. With a tremendous surge the eagle cleared the water and with the crumpled body of its victim went flapping toward the Virginia shore.

Klingel does not identify the species of ducks in the above episode.

Since canvasbacks form large rafts, sometimes numbering in the thousands of birds, one would think that an eagle could fly into such a compact aggregation and easily pick one out. There is not much evidence that this happens. G. Michael Haramis, studying the ecology of the canvasback in the Chesapeake Bay country, watched an eagle make passes at a flock of canvasbacks resting on the water. He said that the canvasbacks showed little concern for the eagle and did not fly or dive as it passed over them. But a nearby flock of Canada geese were much alarmed and took wing when the eagle flew near. From his observations of Chesapeake Bay waterfowl in the last five years, Haramis has concluded that eagles take very few healthy ducks. In the course of his work, he made an interesting photograph of an eagle feeding on a bufflehead near a flock of sleeping canvasbacks.

On February 2, 1936, I was observing birds at Robins Point at the end of the Edgewood Arsenal peninsula, between the Bush and Gunpowder rivers and observed an eagle standing on the ice near a hole kept open by a flock of canvasbacks, mallards, blacks, and whistling swans. During the thirty minutes or so that I watched, neither predator nor prey moved about very much. There was certainly no assault by the eagle at that time.

Other large raptors also prey on waterfowl. When I visited Spesutie Island in the Susquehanna Flats on February 16, 1936, the island was a shooting preserve stocked with upland game but it was also a ducking club. The game keeper at that time was pole trapping hawks and owls. He had just caught six snowy owls, rare winter visitors from the arctic. Most records of snowy owls in Maryland are from the Chesapeake Bay country, suggesting that they are there because of the large waterfowl populations, or also possibly because of the rodent populations of the marshes.

The great black-backed gull, largest of our gulls, is a relatively recent addition to the Bay's avifauna, having gradually extended its range southward from the North Atlantic Coast. Waterfowl biologist G. Michael Haramis has observed that in areas where there is a gathering of canvasbacks, particularly where there is shoreline feeding of corn, the canvasbacks are very tenacious to the feeding site. Great black-backed gulls, taking advantage of this tenacity, sometimes frequent these gathering places to harass the flock hoping to notice a weak or sick bird. A weak bird is easily dispatched by the predator.

Chesapeake Bay is the number one wintering ground of the canvasback and the most important nesting area of the bald eagle on the Atlantic Coast north of Florida. During most of the first half of the twentieth century, there were several hundred active bald eagle nests in the Chesapeake Bay region, and several hundred thousand canvasbacks. Through the 1970s, there were only about sixty active eagle nests and sixty thousand wintering canvasbacks.

9

The Natives

Most waterfowl that winter in the Chesapeake Bay Country breed in Canada and in the northern tier of states. There are only four native species that regularly breed in the Maryland and Virginia sections of the Chesapeake. These are the black duck, blue-winged teal, gadwall, and wood duck. Two additional species have been reported as rare breeders. There have been about a half dozen nesting records of the hooded merganser, most of them in wood duck nest boxes, and there is one record of a green-winged teal having nested in a marsh near Dames Quarter in Somerset County, Maryland (34).

Canada geese and mallards are common nesting birds on some refuges, private sanctuaries, and other places but are not native breeding birds. These two species have been imprinted or are from wing-clipped breeding stock imported from game farms and native breeding areas farther north or west. Frank Kirkwood, author of *A List of the Birds of Maryland* published in 1895, does not name these two species as breeding birds of the state at that time. Also, Mae Thacher Cook did not list them as breeding birds in her *Birds of the Washington, D.C. Region*, published in 1929. Local oologists or egg collectors of the early 1900s did not consider them to be native species. Eggs in their collections came from game bird farms or from the northern breeding grounds. The mute swan is a more recent nonnative waterfowl species that has escaped from captivity and become established as a breeding bird in the Chesapeake Bay area.

Apparently the black duck is the most abundant for the four species of native waterfowl that breed in the Chesapeake Bay country (Figure 87). There seem to be no estimates of the number of native waterfowl that breed there. Stewart and Robbins (17) found a breeding population of 5.3 pairs of black ducks per hundred acres (53 in 1,000 acres) in extensive brackish marshes in southern Dorchester County in 1956. Stotts and Davis (35), who made an intensive study of the breeding biology of the black duck in the general area of Kent Island, Queen Anne's County, Maryland in the 1950s, found as many as 106 nests in one year on Bodkin Island, which is only five acres in size. The authors found active nests as close as 5 feet apart on the ground, and several active nests were found on the same roof of a duck blind.

In their study area, nest locations were as follows: sixty-five percent on the ground in upland areas, mostly in woods, but some also in hay and weedy fields; seventeen percent were in marshes; and nineteen percent on duck blinds. In southern Dorchester and Somerset counties where the marsh acreage is much greater, the percentage of nests in those marshes would be much higher.

Figure 87a. *Right, above,* Nest and eggs of black duck tucked away in big cordgrass marsh, Elliott Island, Dorchester County, Maryland. Photograph: Brooke Meanley. Figure 87b. *Right, below,* Banding a young black duck at Elliott Island, Dorchester County, Maryland. Dorchester marshes have long been known as one of the top black duck and muskrat production areas in North America. Photograph: Brooke Meanley.

145

146

Stotts and Davis (35) found nests in a number of odd locations. Four nests were located in trees, one in an old common grackle nest twelve feet from the ground; and three in old nests of great blue herons seventy to ninety feet above the ground in loblolly pine trees. The roofs rather than seats of duck blinds were generally selected for nest sites because they were covered with cedar or pine branches to help camouflage the blinds.

In one area in 1954, Stotts banded two female black ducks which he trapped while they were on their nests. Both nests were later destroyed by crows, but within three weeks each had constructed a new nest within one hundred yards of the old sites. It is of interest that two years later both females nested within a few yards of their 1954 nests (36).

The nesting season of the black duck begins in mid-March and extends to September for late nesters. However, the nesting peak is in late April. Average clutch size is about ten eggs; and in the Stotts-Davis study, sixty-two percent of the birds produced broods.

The blue-winged teal is a locally common breeding bird in Dorchester and Somerset counties and is occasionally found breeding in some other counties bordering the Bay (Figure 88 & 89).

In *Blackwater* (37) I wrote of the discovery and description of a local breeding population of blue-winged teal in the marshes of Dorchester County, Maryland as follows:

> In the 1932 *Auk*, journal of the American Ornithologists' Union, Oliver Austin of the U.S. Biological Survey reported the first evidence of the nesting of the blue-winged teal in Maryland. Austin's report was based on information obtained in the Blackwater marshes in the period 1929-31. This proved to be an

Figure 88. *Left, above,* Nest and eggs of blue-winged teal in extensive brackish marsh meadow in southern Dorchester County, Maryland, in May. Vegetation is mostly saltmeadow cordgrass (*Spartina patens*). Photograph: Brooke Meanley.
Figure 89. *Left, below,* Female blue-winged teal and brood in marsh near Dames Quarter, Somerset County, Maryland. The blue-winged teal is one of four native waterfowl species that regularly nest in the Chesapeake Bay region. Photograph: Matthew C. Perry, USFWS.

interesting discovery as this small species of waterfowl was thought to be only a spring and fall migrant and occasional winter visitor in the Chesapeake Bay country, with breeding populations originating mainly in the pothole region of the northern prairie states and Prairie Provinces of Canada (particularly Saskatchewan and Manitoba).

Austin recorded the events leading to the discovery of the young and nests of the blue-winged teal at Blackwater: On July 13, 1929, W.G. Tregoe of Cambridge, a warden with the Maryland Game and Inland Fish Commission, found several young ducks that he believed were teal, and whose identification was later confirmed by Talbot Denmead, ornithologist with the U.S. Biological Survey; and canoeing on the Blackwater and Little Blackwater rivers in June and July 1930, Denmead observed several broods of blue-winged teals; then on May 27, 1931, Austin, Tregoe, and others found the first nest and eggs. The nest was located about 200 yards from Shorter's Landing.

At the time of the Blackwater discovery a small population was known to nest in the Louisiana Gulf Coast marshes, and now it was established that a breeding population also existed in the Dorchester County marshes. It is interesting to note that the blue-winged teal no longer nests in Louisiana.

Some years later, in the early 1950s, Robert E. Stewart and John W. Aldrich, ornithologists with the U.S. Fish and Wildlife Service, suspecting that the Chesapeake Bay birds might be morphologically different enough from western or interior

Figure 90. *Right, above,* Nest and eggs of gadwall in salt marsh (*Spartina alterniflora*) in June near Chincoteague, Virginia. The gadwall apparently is a recent addition to the list of breeding birds of the Middle Atlantic States. It was first reported breeding in the Chesapeake Bay country in 1948. An estimated four hundred pairs were reported to be nesting at Chincoteague National Wildlife Refuge in the summer of 1975. Photograph: Brooke Meanley. Figure 91. *Right, below,* Optimum wood duck brood habitat along Nassawango Creek, a tributary of the Pocomoke River, Worcester County, Maryland. Note characteristic flat top of bald cypress tree. Photograph: Brooke Meanley.

Figure 92. Pond used by a pair of wood ducks during the nesting season in southern Dorchester County, Maryland. Their nest was nearby in an old pileated woodpecker nest hole. Photograph: Brooke Meanley.

Figure 93. Francis M. Uhler, waterfowl biologist for over fifty years with the U.S. Fish and Wildlife Service, standing by raccoon-proof wood duck nest box that he developed at the Patuxent Wildlife Research Center near Laurel, Maryland. Photograph: Matthew C. Perry, USFWS.

breeding populations of blue-winged teal to be a distinct subspecies, collected a series of breeding specimens from Dorchester marshes in May, June, and July. Upon comparing them with museum specimens of breeding birds from the interior, it became apparent that Dorchester County specimens were much darker than those from the Midwest and Prairie Provinces of Canada. In the course of their examinations of many specimens from several museums, they found that all breeding blue-winged teal from the Atlantic Coastal region extending from North Carolina to the Maritime Provinces of Canada were much darker than birds from the interior. So, as Stewart and Aldrich state in their paper on the subject, "It is concluded on the basis of the marked color differences and apparent geographical segregation during the breeding season that two recognizable races of blue-winged teal exist which are sufficiently distinct to warrant application of different subspecific names." Thus, the authors described and named their new geographic race or subspecies *Anas discors orphna*, the Atlantic blue-winged teal. The interior subspecies then became known as *Anas discors discors*. The technical terms have the following meanings: *Anas* is Latin for duck; *discors* is Latin for discordant, a reference to the sound made when teal take off in flight; and *orphna* is from the Green *orphnos*, meaning dark or dusky.

The authors indicate that the center of abundance of the Atlantic blue-winged teal breeding population is in the brackish tidal marshes of New Jersey, Delaware, and Maryland, particularly Dorchester County, Maryland, and Delaware Bay marshes of Delaware and New Jersey.

Since the study of speciation and subspeciation in birds is often of little interest or is unknown to the layman, it should be pointed out that many of our species of birds are separated into subspecies or geographic races by ornithologists on the basis of size or color differences, or both. As taxomonic studies of birds continue, museum or university scientists find that not only can some species be separated into distinct races or subspecies, as in the case of the blue-winged teal, but that some can be lumped into a single species. A good example of lumping is our Baltimore oriole, which until 1973 was considered to be a distinct species. But it was found that its western counterpart, Bullock's oriole, intergrades with the Baltimore in the Great Plains States;

Figure 94. Baby wood ducks in nest box. Photograph: Ron E. Shay, Oregon Game Commission.

thus, the two subspecies have been lumped into a single species now known as the northern oriole. So, in this case, instead of having two species of orioles, there are now two subspecies which differ from each other only slightly in plumage markings.

The gadwall seems to be a relatively recent addition to the Chesapeake's native avifauna. The first reported nesting record for the Maryland section of the Chesapeake Bay area was in 1948 when seven pairs were found nesting in a tidal marsh in Somerset County, Maryland near Dames Quarter by Paul Springer and Robert E. Stewart (38). Gadwalls have since been found nesting in Dorchester County and along the Virginia coast at Chincoteague (Figure 90). The nesting period is from early May to late July. Most nesting is in marshes and occasionally in fields near water.

The wood duck is a locally common nesting bird mainly in forest bottomlands, swamps (Figure 91 & 92), and artificial nest boxes (Figure 93, 94, & 95) in the various physiographic provinces in Maryland and Virginia. The nesting season begins in early March, with some broods coming off as late as early September. The peak period of nesting is April through June. D.E. Sutherland estimated that about ten thousand wood ducks nest in Maryland and the same number in Virginia (5). Normal clutch size is about twelve eggs; but there is some "dumping" by hens in other nests, and clutches of two or three dozen eggs occasionally are found in a single nest.

The hooded merganser is characteristically a hole nester like the wood duck (Figure 96), but while the few definite nest records of this species in the Chesapeake Bay country have been in artifical nest boxes, there is evidence of possible nesting in natural cavities or holes in trees at two localities not far from Chesapeake Bay. An adult with young was seen by W.B. Tyrrell near Seneca, Montgom-

Figure 95. *Left,* Baby wood duck jumping from nest box. The mother waits below in the water, vocally coaxing her newly hatched young to jump. Photograph courtesy of Masachusetts Division of Fisheries and Game.

156

ery County, Maryland on May 1, 1954. Seneca is on the Potomac River some fifteen miles above the District of Columbia. There is also a record of an adult with young in the Great Dismal Swamp, a few miles below Norfolk, on April 21, 1976.

Presently, one of the best local waterfowl breeding population areas in the Chesapeake Bay country is the Deal Island Wildlife Management Area in Somerset County, Maryland. On July 3, 1980, ornithologist H.T. Armistead noted the following:

135 black ducks (including six broods),

130 gadwalls (including four broods),

95 blue-winged teals (including seven broods),

65 mallards (probably the progeny of earlier introductions)

and 6 green-winged teals.

Figure 96. *Left,* This photograph taken in eastern Arkansas by Peter J. Van Huizen shows the typical nest site of a hooded merganser and a female leaving the nest. The few nesting records in the Chesapeake Bay country have been of birds using artificial nest boxes.

10

The Decline of Waterfowl Populations

Bird populations in general, including waterfowl, are declining in the face of advancing civilization. With the exception of Canada geese and mallards, most species of waterfowl in the Chesapeake Bay country have declined substantially in the last twenty-five years (from an estimated eight hundred thousand to three hundred thousand dabblers and divers in the Maryland section).

Several species are "close to the edge," where disastrous weather conditions on the breeding or wintering grounds for several years in a row could conceivably seriously jeopardize those populations. A case in point is the Atlantic brant, and also the greater snow goose populations. Both populations winter along the Middle Atlantic Coast and breed in the subarctic and arctic. Flooding on the breeding grounds and freezes on the wintering grounds have in some years reduced those populations to dangerously low levels.

In the severe winter of 1977, one of the coldest on record, many brant perished, especially in the more northern part of their winter range. In the New Jersey coastal area, fifty thousand were estimated to have died. Because of the devastating 1977 winter, the following fall the entire Atlantic brant population was down to fifty-five thousand birds. Prior to the 1977 winter freeze-up, the 1976 winter population was estimated at one hundred fifteen thousand birds. The winter of 1978 was somewhat of a repeat of 1977, but with January temperatures averaging four or five degrees warmer. Yet there were reports of an estimated ten thousand brants dying in New Jersey.

The total population of greater snow geese in the fall of 1977 was about one hundred fifty thousand birds. They fared better than the brant during the freeze of 1977, because most of the population winters a little farther south along the coast, mainly in Virginia and North Carolina.

The reduction in the number of wintering black ducks in the Maryland section of Chesapeake Bay from an average population of 129,700 in the period 1953-58, to 18,000 in 1980, is an alarming trend, and can possibly be attributed to hunting (legal and illegal), illegal trapping, and pesticides. Ralph Palmer, editor of the *Handbook of North American Birds* (3), notes:

> The Black eats more, and more varied protein food (small animal life) than, for example, the Mallard; this may result in a higher intake of long-residual pesticides which, in turn, occur widely in Black Ducks and their eggs. These may influence overall numbers, but their effects remain unknown.

The well-known decline of the canvasback in historic times probably began two hundred years ago. The most delectable of waterfowl, the canvasback was the principal target of the market and sport hunter. Dr. John C. Phillips, former Associate Curator of Birds in the Museum of Comparative Zoology at Harvard College points out what Audubon and other early ornithologists had been witnessing. Writing in his four-volume work, *A Natural History of the Ducks*, published in 1925 (4), Dr. Phillips states:

> The famous fresh- and brackish-water bays of the upper Chesapeake, from Havre de Grace to Baltimore, as well as the lower James River were once the greatest wintering grounds of the

160

The Decline of Waterfowl Populations

Canvasback on the Atlantic Coast, and up to twenty-five or thirty years ago they seem in that famed region to have exceeded any other species in numbers. The tremendous persecution which went on there both by night and day in waters that were easily accessible for shooting resulted in a steady diminution long before the time of Wilson and Audubon.

Phillips sights a record of a hunter during the 1846-47 hunting season shooting 7,000 canvasbacks. In the late 1800s and early 1900s, bags of 100 canvasbacks a day were not uncommon for the market gunner. It was at least partly due to hunting pressure that canvasback populations dwindled from several million birds two hundred years ago to estimates of a half million birds in the 1970s.

Unrestricted market and sport shooting continued until prohibitive laws were enacted in 1918. But even before market gunning and unlimited bag limits were curbed, other factors were contributing to the decline of canvasback populations. Perhaps the two most important factors were the reclamation of vast sections of the northern prairie nesting grounds for agricultural purposes and drought during the nesting season.

In "Potholes—Going, Going . . .," a chapter in the U.S. Department of Interior's *Waterfowl Tomorrow* (39), Robert G. Burwell and Lawson G. Sugden state that more than a million acres of waterfowl breeding habitat have been lost to reclamation projects. They also note that:

> The waterfowl continued to thrive when the early immigrants came to the northern prairies to plow the soil. A change came in the late 1800s. New kinds of machinery increased the amount of work a farmer could do and the land he could till. He drained the potholes to increase his acreage. Reclamation of potholes began in the rich soils of the Midwest—first in Iowa, then Nebraska, Minnesota, the Dakotas, and Canada. As drainage became more complicated, judicial drainage districts were established. Everyone seemed to want to get water off the land faster and faster.

Art Hawkins, waterfowl biologist with the U.S. Fish and Wildlife Service in the northern prairie "duck factory" says, strike two on the nesting ground comes from drought. Several biologists are of the opinion that the canvasback population has never fully recovered from the droughts of the early 1930s.

In the chapter "Prairie Potholes and Marshes" in *Waterfowl Tomorrow* (39), Allen G. Smith, Jerome H. Stoudt, and J. Bernard Gollop wrote of the effects of drought on waterfowl breeding grounds:

> Drought is the greatest single disaster that can overtake a waterfowl population in our prairies. Vast areas of grasslands may lose all potholes and lakes except the ones fed by irrigation water or springs. In a series of drought years, like those during the late fifties and early sixties, even the parklands suffer. Breeding populations drop to a fraction of normal, and brood production falls accordingly. Plant and animal food disappears as potholes dry up, and ducks are forced into new, strange, and often unsuitable areas outside the prairies.
>
> Thousands of pairs of ducks of all species failed to nest at all in 1959 and 1961. Large concentrations remained on breeding grounds on permanent lakes. They were still there until mid-June, when many moved southward, even into southern California, at a time when they ordinarily would have been in Canada and the Northern States. Several successive drought years can reduce the number of hens that raise broods to about half that of good years.

The recent northern extension of the range of the raccoon into the breeding grounds has added to the woes of nesting canvasbacks and other prairie ducks. Not only are nests destroyed by raccoons, foxes, minks, and crows, but female ducks are sometimes killed on their nests by some of those predators. This probably is one of the factors responsible for the disparate sex ratio favoring males in the prairie ducks.

When the canvasback leaves the breeding grounds on the fall flight to its winter home, the countdown begins. The hunting season is earlier on the northern prairies in order to take advantage of the birds as they pass through, and before they leave the area completely. Thus, the hunting season may have opened not long

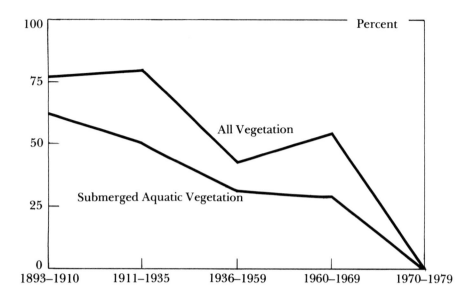

Figure 97. Percent vegetation eaten by canvasbacks during five periods, 1893–1979. From Matthew C. Perry, USFWS.

164

after the young of the year, or immatures, have had a chance to test their wings and face a new experience, the onslaught of the hunter.

Numerous hunting surveys by waterfowl biologists have demonstrated that juveniles and also females are more vulnerable to shooting than are males. David P. Olsen, who has conducted studies on the differential vulnerability of male and female canvasbacks to hunting, has indicated that females are more vulnerable than males to both decoy and pass shooting. Females and immatures, "tend to respond to decoys by flying right in and landing or crossing low over the decoys, but the adult males tend to circle at greater distances, and land in the decoys less often than females and or juveniles (40)."

Biologist Aelred Geis of the U.S. Fish and Wildlife Service found from an analysis of band recoveries of canvasbacks that immatures had an annual mortality rate of seventy-seven percent compared to an adult mortality rate of forty-one percent; and that in a winter sample from Louisiana, males had a mortality rate of thirty-five percent and females, forty-eight percent (41).

In addition to mortality from gunners, canvasbacks and other divers encounter a plethora of other problems on the wintering grounds. Submerged aquatic plants, formerly an abundant food source, are presently in short supply, and where they once made up about eighty to ninety percent of the canvasback's diet, now comprise less than twenty percent in the Chesapeake Bay area (see Figure 97). Clams and other shellfish, which have always been a part of the canvasback's diet, are now the mainstay. What effect, if any, this change in diet has had on canvasback populations or numbers is not known but is being examined by state and federal wildlife biologists. It is, however, of interest and perhaps significant that canvasback, redhead, and wigeon populations have declined along with submerged aquatic vegetation in Chesapeake Bay; whereas population increases of canvasbacks and redheads have been noted

Figure 98. *Left,* Whistling swan—victim of an oil spill. Photograph: Matthew C. Perry, USFWS.

Waterfowl of the Chesapeake Bay Country

in areas of North America that still have an abundance of underwater plants.

An important cause of mortality is the ingestion of lead shot. Canvasbacks and other divers are probably more susceptible to lead poisoning than dabblers or surface feeding ducks, since the divers obtain most of their food from the bottom. In his study of the food habits of diving ducks Cottam reported that ninety-six lead shot were found in a canvasback's stomach. The estimated annual mortality from lead poisoning is between two and three percent, according to Frank Bellrose. With the size of the present continental waterfowl population, there would be a mortality of about two million birds.

Oil spills are another cause of waterfowl mortality (Figure 98). Since Chesapeake and Delaware bays are waterways to several of the largest seaports along the Atlantic Coast, vast shipments of oil are constantly in transit through these waters. According to Matthew C. Perry, between January 1, 1973 and December 31, 1977 there were fourteen major oil spills in the Delaware River during the period October 15-March 15. The ruddy duck was the species most affected.

As a result of an oil spill in the Virginia section of Chesapeake Bay on February 1, 1976, from 15,000 to 50,000 birds were estimated to have died. Among some of the casualties were 2,980 horned grebes, 851 oldsquaws, 126 surf scoters, 88 ruddy ducks, 58 loons, 20 black scoters, 16 scaups, 9 canvasbacks, and 3 black ducks.

The illegal hunting and trapping of waterfowl will always be with us, and the canvasback will usually be a prime candidate. Since

Figure 99. *Right,* Radiograph of a live healthy adult male canvasback with nine embedded shot. This was the most shot ever found in a live canvasback during a three-year study to determine the incidence of embedded shot in this species. The results indicated high levels of shot during years of restrictive hunting regulations for the canvasback. Most shot would have come from illegal hunting. Photograph: Matthew C. Perry, USFWS.

166

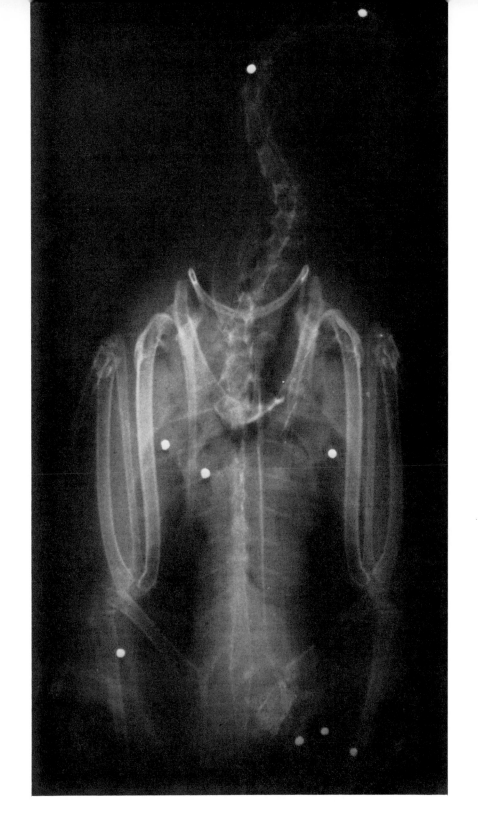

167

Waterfowl of the Chesapeake Bay Country

Chesapeake Bay winters more canvasbacks than any other single area, and for the reason that they are highest on the list of the waterfowl hunter and the epicure, the Bay area usually has more illegal hunting and trapping of ducks than any other section of the United States, with the possible exception of coastal Louisiana.

Matthew C. Perry, who has X-rayed many live canvasbacks that he trapped in the course of banding operations in the Bay, has found that a number of them had lead shot embedded in their bodies (Figure 99) during closed hunting seasons. This of course points to illegal hunting. Perry believes that today such illegal hunting is the greatest single threat to the canvasback.

The canvasback has been characterized as a "boom or bust" species. The "boom" days may be gone. Today the canvasback appears to be precariously holding its own.

THE LABRADOR DUCK

The Labrador duck is the only species of waterfowl that has occurred in the Chesapeake Bay country and is now extinct. The last specimen was taken in 1875 on Long Island. There are no definite sight records beyond that year. Ornithologist D.G. Elliott noted that between 1860 and 1870 he saw a number of females and young males in New York City markets, but that adult males were quite rare. Elliott's observations would seem to indicate that the handsome black and white males were by then the special object of collectors.

The Labrador duck was so named because it was thought to nest along the Labrador coast. It was known to be a bird mainly of the North Atlantic Coast, though a few casually drifted as far south as Chesapeake Bay. It was often reported in the markets of Boston, New York, and Philadelphia. John James Audubon mentions seeing it in markets in Baltimore in 1838 and 1843, and in the Virginia section of Chesapeake Bay. Specimens in Philadelphia markets apparently came from Delaware Bay and the coast of New Jersey.

Many specimens in museums are from Long Island where this sea duck was reported to be common in winter. Audubon's figures of the Labrador duck in *Birds of America* were based on specimens

168

The Decline of Waterfowl Populations

given to him by the statesman, Daniel Webster, who took them during a hunting trip at Martha's Vineyard.

The cause of its extinction is somewhat of a mystery. It was not a gourmet's delight, and although it appeared in markets with other game, there is no evidence that it was slaughtered in great numbers for food. It is thought that it may have been persecuted on the nesting grounds along with eiders whose nests were pilfered for their eggs and down by Indians, Eskimos, and feather merchants from New England.

11
Hunting the Canvasback in the Old Days

The upper Chesapeake Bay, and particularly the Susquehanna Flats, has, until recent times, been known as the most famous hunting ground of the canvasback. The pioneer ornithologists John James Audubon and Alexander Wilson were the first prominent naturalists to write about the canvasback of the Chesapeake Bay Country. In *Birds of America*, published in 1840 (42), Audubon states that

> The Chesapeake Bay with its tributary streams, has from its discovery, been known as the greatest resort of waterfowl in the United States. This has depended upon the profusion of their food, which is accessible on the immense flats or shoals that are found near the mouth of the Susquehanna, along the entire length of the North-East and Elk Rivers, and on the shores of the bay and connecting streams as far south as York and James Rivers.

Alexander Wilson, whose career began earlier than Audubon's, but overlapped it, was also an author and illustrator of birds.

Waterfowl of the Chesapeake Bay Country

Audubon's paintings were more artistic and his career more illustrious, thus he is better known; but the contribution of the two to the science of ornithology was of equal importance. Wilson described the canvasback, giving it the scientific name *Anas valisineria*. *Anas*, the generic name, Latin for duck, was later replaced by the zoological taxonomists with *Aythya*, Greek for waterfowl. The specific name *valisineria* (misspelled by Wilson), is from the scientific name of the submerged aquatic plant wild celery (*Vallisneria americana*).

In volume 8 of his *American Ornithology* (1804-1814), Wilson identifies the canvasback with the Chesapeake Bay country by reference to hunting:

> The Canvas-back duck arrives in the United States from the north about the middle of October, a few descend to the Hudson and Delaware, but the great body of these birds resort to the numerous rivers belonging to and in the neighborhood of the Chesapeake Bay, particularly the Susquehannah, the Patapsco, Potomac, and James Rivers. . . . At the Susquehannah they are called *Canvas-backs*, on the Potomac *White-backs*, and on the James river *Sheldrakes*. They are seldom found at a great distance up any of these rivers or even in the salt water bay; but in that particular part of the tide water where a certain grass-like plant grows, on the roots of which they feed. This plant which is said to be a species of *Valisineria*, grows in fresh water shoals of from seven to nine feet (but never where these are occasionally dry) in long narrow grass-like blades of four or five feet in length; the root is white, and has some resemblance to small celery.
>
> The Canvas-back in the rich juicy tenderness of its flesh, and its delicacy of flavor, stands unrivalled by the whole of its tribe in this or perhaps any other quarter of the world. These

Figure 100. *Right,* The battery gun, *left,* and the big gun were used in the old days by pot or market gunners. Before they became illegal, about 1918, these guns were mounted to shoot off the bows of skiffs. They were usually used at night, and as many as one hundred ducks were sometimes killed with a single shot. Photograph: Matthew C. Perry, USFWS.

172

173

Waterfowl of the Chesapeake Bay Country

killed in the waters of the Chesapeake are generally esteemed superior to all others, doubtless from the great abundance of their favorite food which the rivers produce. At our public dinners, hotels and particular entertainments, the Canvas-backs are universal favorites. They not only grace but dignify the table, and their very name conveys to the imagination of the eager epicure the most comfortable and exhilarating ideas. Hence on such occasions it has not been uncommon to pay from one to three dollars a pair for these ducks, and indeed, at such times, if they can they must be had, whatever may be the price.

Audubon's and Wilson's story of the canvasback on the upper Chesapeake takes us back one hundred fifty years, but this most esteemed of waterfowl has been around for at least ten thousand years. There are fossil remains of canvasbacks from the Pleistocene epoch discovered in Alaska, Washington, California, Iowa, and Illinois. The earliest known waterfowl decoys were made for hunting the canvasback. These early examples were found by scientists in a cave in Nevada. According to Roger Tory Peterson in his book *Birds Over America* (43): "There in the rubble of a pre-Paiute civilization called the 'tule eaters,' they found some bundles of tule reeds carefully fashioned into the unmistakeable form of Canvasbacks. ." Scientists were able to determine that these decoys had been fashioned over two thousand years ago!

Canvasback hunting on the Susquehanna Flats reached its peak in the late 1800s and early part of this century., There were two types of hunters: the sportsman who was out primarily for the enjoyment of it, and the market or pothunter who made a business of it.

The standard method of hunting canvasbacks employed by the sportsman and some market hunters in the old days was the sinkbox. The sinkbox was a rectangular box large enough for a man to lie down in, with wide wings covered with canvas and weighted down with iron decoys so the level of the rig was just a few inches above the surface of the water. Surrounding this apparatus were placed a hundred or more wooden decoys.

Some pothunters lived on the Susquehanna estuary in flat-bottomed sailboats during the entire ducking season. They used an

174

Hunting the Canvasback in the Old Days

armament of swivel guns (large bore guns attached to the bow of a boat), battery guns of eight or ten barrels arranged in fan-shape, and all firing simultaneously (Figure 100). Much of the pothunting was done at night with a light. Because canvasbacks assembled in large rafts, thousands were slaughtered. Such wholesale killing of ducks by these methods was outlawed in 1918. Also, the sinkbox was no longer allowed after 1935.

Another method in the old days of hunting canvasbacks on the Flats was known as tolling. It has been said that tolling had its origin a couple of hundred years ago in England; and the idea came from someone watching a raft of ducks swimming toward the shore apparently lured by a red fox that was trotting along the shoreline. From that time on a dog was used to lure the ducks shoreward. Diving ducks, especially canvasbacks, redheads, and scaup are more curious than other waterfowl and were quite readily tolled in by a Chesapeake Bay retriever or almost any well trained dog.

One such interesting article on the subject by G.L. Hopper appeared in a 1928 issue of the *Maryland Conservationist* (44) and was based on the author's experiences on the Susquehanna Flats. The title of the article is "Old Bob of Spesutie Island." Old Bob was a Chesapeake Bay retriever.

> At tolling old Bob was unexcelled. We would saunter along the shore of the island until we located a raft of ducks, within a half mile of shore. Then if conditions were favorable we would hide behind an old log or a pile of driftwood, as nearly opposite the ducks as possible. Bob was then coaxed into the hiding place and a red bandana, borrowed from old Aunt Melissa for the occasion, was made fast about midship of Bob's tail. When the bandana was made fast and secure, out would bound Old Bob, delighted to begin tolling. He would begin about fifty yards above us or below us, running belly deep in the surf, barking at the top of his voice, then turn at about fifty yards, keeping up the performance until the ducks' attention was attracted. As the ducks swam in toward the shore Bob worked back upon the shore until he was to our rear some ten or fifteen yards, always on the bounce and barking as loud as he could. I have had ducks come into the very edge of the surf; then, with a steady rest and aim that never failed, we would knock over five or six at a shot, sometimes more. . . .

175

Waterfowl of the Chesapeake Bay Country

Some tolling dogs had a red flag tied to their tails in the daytime and a white flag at night.

Much of the hunting of canvasbacks during the late 1800s and early 1900s was along the west side of the upper Bay between the mouth of the Susquehanna and the mouth of the Patapsco. Along this stretch there are several rivers and creeks flowing into the Bay that are separated by peninsulas. Some of the early hunters referred to this section of the bay shore as "The Necks." Because "The Necks" were located close to Baltimore and Philadelphia, and otherwise strategically located for hunting canvasbacks and other waterfowl, this area was especially good for pass shooting as the birds flew over the peninsulas or were whipped into the coves in stormy weather.

Among the best areas for shooting canvasbacks south of the Flats toward Baltimore were at Abbey and Leges Points at the mouth of Bush River, at Robins Point at the end of Gunpowder River Neck, and at Back River Neck near Baltimore Harbor.

One of the earliest well known ducking clubs close to Baltimore was known as Marshy Point and was located on Saltpetre and Dundee Creeks, only about fifteen miles from City Hall. Hunting there goes back to the 1850s, and it is said that at that time the majority of ducks shot were canvasbacks and redheads. Other well known hunting clubs close to Baltimore in the late 1800s and early 1900s were Carroll's Island, Benjies Point, Grace's Quarter, Bowley's Quarters, and Miller's Island (Figure 101 & 102).

I had often heard of duck shooting at Miller's Island from my friends Percy Blogg and Talbot Denmead, members of the club. Perce, as he was known among his friends, wrote an interesting chapter about hunting at the island in his book entitled *There Are No Dull Dark Days* (45).

> Within big-gun range of Sparrows Point, with its great furnaces and smoking stacks, and lying just off the mouth of Back River, there's an island . . . in fact, two islands for now it has become separated by the ravages of the nor'easters bringing with them heavy ice floes and high seas until a shallow channel has been cut between the once long strip of land. While the chart shows "Hart" and "Millers" islands, it is more popularly known only as Millers.

176

Figure 101. The Miller's Island Ducking Club in the early 1900s. Photograph courtesy of Percy Blogg.

Figure 102. Members of the club. Percy Blogg, well-known Baltimore sportsman-naturalist is second from left (and smiling). Photograph courtesy of Mr. Blogg.

Hunting the Canvasback in the Old Days

and seasons and bag limits were established. From 1918-29, the bag limit on ducks was twenty-five. By 1932, the limit was fifteen ducks with special restrictions on canvasbacks. There was no hunting of canvasbacks for the first time in the fall and winter of 1936-37. As waterfowl populations have declined, bag limits have decreased and by the decade of the 1970s, in most years the season was closed on canvasbacks, which showed the most marked decline of the various duck species.

When they see a raft of thirty or forty thousand canvasbacks on some lakes and waters during the migration period or on some embayment on the wintering ground, there are still hunters today that cannot understand why there are not more liberal regulations on hunting these birds. What these hunters may not realize is that they are seeing an appreciable segment of the continental population of that species, which in recent years has totaled only four to five hundred thousand birds. Compare this number with a continental population of nine million mallards.

Let us hope that there will always be a canvasback, the king of waterfowl, a most handsome bird, and a gourmet's delight. An example of the high esteem with which it is regarded by the waterfowl hunter is well illustrated by a tale told to Hulbert Footner (46) by Dr. Hugh H. Young, a distinguished surgeon at Johns Hopkins Hospital in the first half of the 1900s and an ardent duck hunter.

> Upon his return from a duck shoot he was apportioning the game to be sent to his friends. The bag contained only a few of the prized Canvasbacks. There was a distinguished confrere that Dr. Young wished to honor, but he thought: Pshaw! Dr. _____ is completely immersed in his specialty; he wouldn't know the difference between Canvasback and Mallard. Yet something warned Dr. Young that he had better send the Canvasback and he did. A few days later Dr. _____ met him with a beaming smile. "Young," he cried, "I suspected with the first mouthful I took that those were canvasback you sent me, and I asked for one of the heads to make sure. They had been thrown out so I took a poker and rummaged in the garbage can until I turned one up. And, by God! they *were* Canvasback!"

12

Where to See Waterfowl in the Chesapeake Bay Country

In parts of the foregoing text I have briefly mentioned various wildlife refuges in reference to the distribution of waterfowl in the Chesapeake Bay country. While it is obvious that these are among the places to see a variety and abundance of waterfowl, there also are other vantage points, as seen by the various local areas selected for annual Christmas Counts. Waterfowl concentration areas where such counts are made include among others Annapolis, Point Lookout at the mouth of the Potomac River, Kent County near the mouth of the Chester River, St. Michaels, and Crisfield in Maryland and Newport News, Craney Island near Portsmouth, Hopewell south of Richmond, and Cape Charles in Virginia.

Since many wildlife refuges are located in marshy areas, they are among the best places to see dabbling ducks and geese. But the diving ducks tend to concentrate in large bodies of water, and to see such divers as the scoters, scaups, and redheads, one sometimes has to visit the Bay proper and some of its larger estuaries, particularly the lower reaches of some of the larger rivers.

183

Waterfowl of the Chesapeake Bay Country

EASTERN SHORE OF MARYLAND
Blackwater National Wildlife Refuge

Blackwater is located on the Eastern Shore of Maryland in southern Dorchester County, about ten miles below Cambridge. From Baltimore, Washington, and Annapolis, take U.S. route 50, which runs through Cambridge and continue east a short distance to route 16 and the sign directing one to the Refuge. Continue on route 16 to Church Creek and turn south on route 335 to the Refuge. Located along the Big and Little Blackwater rivers, the refuge was established in 1933. It has approximately fourteen thousand acres, mainly of marshland, loblolly pine woods, hardwood swamps, freshwater ponds, and agricultural land. It is one of the best areas to see Canada and lesser snow geese at close range. Canadas (Figure 103) begin arriving in early October and snow geese in the latter part of the month and in November. Both species often feed on grasses near the visitor center. The main wildlife drive goes through marshland and by impoundments where most of the species of dabblers or surface-feeding ducks can be seen in the fall, winter, or early spring. A few canvasbacks and other diving ducks, mergansers, and whistling swans sometimes frequent the freshwater impoundments. Also, one should drive east of the visitors center to the blacktop road that runs south for about five miles through extensive brackish marshes to the Blackwater River bridge at Shorter's Wharf at the village of Robbins to see more marsh ducks.

Hooper and Elliott Islands

With the largest marshland acreage in Maryland and with its bordering embayments, southern Dorchester County is probably the best all-around area in the Chesapeake Bay country for seeing a variety of waterfowl. In addition to Blackwater Refuge, two other areas are conveniently located for those seeking good vantage points for waterfowl. Travelling west a short distance from the visitors center to route 335, follow the road south to *Hooper Island*, which is connected by a bridge and causeway to the mainland. This

184

Figure 103. "Putting on the brakes." This photograph of a group of Canada geese coming in for a landing is unique in showing how the feathers on the side of the breast, along with the wings and feet, are extended to slow the birds down. Photograph: Luther Goldman, USFWS.

is a good location from which to see diving ducks either in Honga River, Tar Bay, and Chesapeake Bay, all of which border the island.

Southeast of Blackwater, lying between Fishing Bay and the Nanticoke River is *Elliott Island*, a vast brackish marshland through which a hardtop road travels for ten miles. The marsh is pocked with dozens of ponds, habitats for dabblers, hooded mergansers, and some divers. A part of the road borders Fishing Bay. To reach Elliott Island, follow U.S. route 50 east from Cambridge to Vienna, enter the village on the right side of the highway, and take the road leading south to Elliott.

Deal Island Wildlife Management Area

One of the finest waterfowl management areas maintained by the State of Maryland Department of Natural Resources is the *Deal Island Wildlife Management Area*, located in Somerset County, Maryland, on the lower Eastern Shore, about ten miles west of Princess Anne. The area is close to Tangier Sound on the west, Monie Bay on the north and Manokin River on the south. From Salisbury go south on U.S. route 13 to Princess Anne and then west on route 363, which goes through the wildlife management area. There are several roads out into the marshes, the best is along a dike that leads south at the post office in the village of Dames Quarter. The wildlife management area is actually a part of the mainland, but beyond a short distance is a bridge over to Deal Island, a good vantage point for seeing diving ducks out in the large bodies of water.

Eastern Neck National Wildlife Refuge and Remington Farms

The best area for waterfowl in the northern part of the Chesapeake is *Eastern Neck National Wildlife Refuge* which is near the mouth of the Chester River. Close by is *Remington Farms*, a private wildlife management area open to the public from February 1 to October 10 during daylight hours. The Eastern Neck-Remington Farms section is presently the most important concentration area for Canada geese in the Chesapeake Bay country. According to the Eastern Neck Refuge leaflet:

186

Most waterfowl begin arriving in early October. Their numbers reach a peak in November. Whistling swan, Canada goose, bufflehead, wigeon, pintail, mallard, black duck, canvasback, and scaup are the principal waterfowl using the refuge. The presence of sea ducks such as the oldsquaw and white-winged scoter makes the refuge more interesting. Most waterfowl leave the refuge by early April.

Eastern Neck Refuge and Remington Farms are located near Rock Hall, in Kent County, and can be reached taking route 20 west from Chestertown.

WESTERN SHORE OF MARYLAND

Annapolis

In the Annapolis area of the Western Shore, there are good vantage points where canvasbacks and other divers can be observed north of the Chesapeake Bay Bridge at *Sandy Point State Park*, and south of the bridge by taking route 2 and route 665 to *Bay Ridge*. Nearby at Annapolis, waterfowl can often be observed at the U.S. Naval Academy, located at the mouth of the Severn River. The Academy grounds are open to the public. Herring Bay, about 18 miles south of Annapolis, is an inundation along Chesapeake Bay where divers can be seen from North Beach. The area can be reached by taking route 2 from Annapolis and route 4 from Upper Marlboro.

Baltimore Harbor

Baltimore usually has several flocks of canvasbacks and ruddies throughout the winter, often with an increase in those two species in late February and March as waterfowl begin moving up the Bay with the advent of spring migration. Eighteen species of waterfowl were reported there on the December 31, 1979 Christmas Count. One of the best points from which to see waterfowl in the harbor is at Broening Park, next to South Baltimore General Hospital. To reach Broening Park from Baltimore, take Hanover Street south, and after crossing the Hanover Street Bridge, the park will be on the left. Coming from the south toward Baltimore on the Baltimore-Washington Parkway, shortly after entering the city limits, turn off at Waterview Avenue, which leads toward Broening Park and South Baltimore General Hospital. Fort McHenry, in Baltimore Harbor is also a public access area from which waterfowl can sometimes be seen.

VIRGINIA

Hog Island Wildlife Refuge

Hog Island Wildlife Refuge is a state wildlife area on the south shore of the James River, across from Jamestown. It can be reached from the Richmond-Petersburg Turnpike (I-95), by taking route 10 east to Bacon's Castle, then turning north on route 650 about five miles to the refuge. It is located near the Surry Nuclear Power Plant. A variety of waterfowl occur at the refuge, especially geese and dabblers; and the main road onto the refuge is a dike high above the artificial impoundments from which waterfowl can easily be observed.

Presquile National Wildlife Refuge

Located along the upper tidal section of the James River, near Hopewell and a few miles below Richmond, the refuge is accessible by private boat or refuge-operated ferry which runs at irregular intervals. For this reason, the refuge manager should be notified of a visit in advance. Address is Box 658, Hopewell, Virginia 23860. A variety of dabblers and sometimes snow geese occur at the refuge.

Back Bay National Wildlife Refuge

This refuge is located about fifteen miles south of the mouth of Chesapeake Bay along the coast and below Norfolk and Virginia Beach. It can be reached via Sandbridge which is about five miles north of the refuge. Back Bay is one of the best waterfowl areas in Virginia, and is a major concentration area for greater snow geese.

Chincoteague National Wildlife Refuge

Chincoteague Refuge is located on the ocean side of the Eastern Shore of Virginia, a short distance south of the Maryland line.

188

Most of the refuge is across a creek on Assateague Island that fronts on the ocean. From U.S. route 13 that runs down the center of the Eastern Shore of Virginia, about five miles south of the Maryland line, take route 175 east to Chincoteague. The long causeway across the marshes and creeks leading to the village of Chincoteague has turnouts from which waterfowl can be observed in the winter. After crossing the bridge that leads into the village of Chincoteague, make a left turn and follow the signs to the refuge. Greater snow geese, Atlantic brant, and many dabblers and divers winter in the area.

Saxis Marsh

This is a state refuge located just below the Maryland line on the Chesapeake Bay side of the Eastern Shore of Virginia. It borders Pocomoke Sound and part of Chesapeake Bay and is an important dabbler duck habitat. Turn west off U.S. route 13 to route 695 and follow the signs.

Chesapeake Bay-Bridge Tunnel

Leading from the lower end of the Eastern Shore of Virginia at Cape Charles to Norfolk across the mouth of Chesapeake Bay, the Bridge-Tunnel has several turnouts where cars can stop and observers may see some of the lesser known waterfowl, the king eider and harlequin duck. Oldsquaws and scoters also occur regularly in these waters.

Craney Island

Also in the Norfolk region is the Craney Island disposal area near Portsmouth and the mouth of the James River. The area can be reached by going to Portsmouth, going north on route 17 to Coleman Nurseries, turning right on Cedar Road to Churchland Junior High School, then turning left to Rivershore Drive and noting signs to Craney Island. For weekend visits, contact the Army Corps of Engineers in the area ahead of time. The Craney Island landfill or disposal area is one of the best for seeing many of the dabblers and shorebirds. However, at times the area is relatively dry, thus it is best to contact local birders to find out about conditions there.

Waterfowl of the Chesapeake Bay Country

Ocean City and Bombay Hook Refuge

Not far from Chesapeake Bay is Ocean City, Maryland, on the coast of the Atlantic, and Bombay Hook National Wildlife Refuge on Delaware Bay, both better than average waterfowl areas. At Ocean City, check the ocean from the beach, boardwalk, or one of the piers, the inlet at the south end of the boardwalk that separates Ocean City from Assateague Island, and Sinepuxent Bay behind the town. Snow geese and brant usually occur at Ocean City along with the variety of ducks.

To reach Bombay Hook Refuge, take route 6 east of Smyrna, Delaware, and then go south on route 9 and follow the signs. Snow geese and Canadas winter at Bombay Hook, and numerous dabblers are seen at the several impoundments.

Pope's Creek and Point Lookout

Two observation points along the lower Potomac, of interest because of waterfowl and for other reasons are Pope's Creek in Westmoreland County, Virginia and Point Lookout in St. Mary's County, Maryland. Pope's Creek, a small estuary off the Potomac lies beside George Washington's birthplace, "Wakefield," and often has good numbers of canvasbacks, scaups, whistling swan, and other waterfowl. The waterfowl may be in the Creek or along the Potomac where they can be seen from a bluff at Washington's birthplace. Pope's Creek on the "Northern Neck" of Virginia, can be reached by taking route 3 east of U.S. route 301. Just beyond Washington's birthplace is Westmoreland State Park, with a high bluff overlooking a section of the Potomac, also a good vantage point for observing scaups and canvasbacks. A short distance down the Potomac from Pope's Creek and Westmoreland State Park are the mouths of Nomini Creek and Currioman Bay a frequent loafing and feeding place of divers.

Point Lookout, at the confluence of the Potomac and Chesapeake Bay, is in the general area where the first settlers of Maryland came ashore. A Christmas Count is conducted in this area each year because of the relative high numbers of divers, particularly scoters, canvasbacks, buffleheads, and common goldeneyes. Route 235 south from Lexington Park leads to Point Lookout and the mouth of the Potomac.

190

Figure 104. A raft of canvasbacks on the Bay. Photograph: G. Michael Haramis, USFWS.

Appendix 1

JANUARY INVENTORY*
(Chesapeake Bay and Maryland-Virginia Coast)

Species	1979	1980
Mallard	70,824	69,966
Black Duck	51,324	53,968
Gadwall	7,825	21,183
American Wigeon	3,924	13,432
Blue-winged Teal	—	—
Green-winged Teal	2,582	3,600
Northern Shoveler	3,618	1,088
Common Pintail	6,440	8,943
Wood Duck	525	—
Fulvous Whistling Duck	100	—
Redhead	8,701	10,369
Canvasback	68,966	31,154
Scaups (2 species)	28,727	23,367
Ring-necked Duck	3,031	4,064
Common Goldeneye	16,381	4,300
Bufflehead	22,858	19,634
Ruddy Duck	24,398	14,984
Oldsquaw	13,975	5,124
Scoters (3 species)	21,096	17,506
Mergansers (3 species)	4,683	5,247
Lesser Snow Goose	550	1,056
Greater Snow Goose	36,804	59,354
Canada Goose	634,484	562,477
Atlantic Brant	1,800	10,706
Whistling Swan	44,183	41,334
European Mute Swan	21	100
American Coot	6,149	15,115
	1,083,969	998,071

*data from U.S. Fish and Wildlife Service

Appendix 2

**DISTRIBUTION AND RELATIVE ABUNDANCE OF WATERFOWL
IN SELECTED LOCALITIES OF CHESAPEAKE BAY**

(population averages, 1973-77 Christmas Counts)

Species	Annapolis-Gibson Island	Lower Kent County	St. Michaels
Whistling Swan	511	1,225	4,423
Canada Goose	3,130	100,684	53,310
Atlantic Brant	0	1	0.6
White-fronted Goose	0	0	0
Snow Goose	0.2	4	141
Mallard	895	1,582	713
Black Duck	171	422	317
Gadwall	40	10	0
Common Pintail	0.4	141	19
Blue-winged Teal	0	0	0
Green-winged Teal	5	8	0
American Wigeon	138	7	6
Northern Shoveler	0.4	7	0
Wood Duck	1	2	0
Redhead	64	24	13
Ring-necked Duck	3	12	0.2
Canvasback	8,394	1,693	3,450
Greater Scaup	2,505	78	2
Lesser Scaup	1,184	435	165
Common Goldeneye	805	248	465
Bufflehead	347	120	1,769
Oldsquaw	548	297	2,052
White-winged Scoter	14	217	972
Surf Scoter	212	1	114
Black Scoter	5	17	39
Ruddy Duck	1,623	107	1,300
Hooded Merganser	10	12	0
Common Merganser	6	8	0
Red-breasted Merganser	5	9	25

Pt. Lookout	Southern Dorchester County	Crisfield	Newport News, Va.
1,051	636	112	5
1,555	30,774	2,023	32
0	0	110	25
0	0.2	0	0
2	1,309	6	0
136	1,296	212	221
73	736	568	13
3	4	1	9
0	190	5	0.6
1	9	1	12
0.4	44	15	22
5	14	2	795
0	16	2	7
2	0.4	3	9
33	114	33	28
0	0.4	1	16
2,218	673	1,052	667
560	8	200	4
134	8	22	240
486	41	179	584
806	140	524	268
2,922	18	243	92
626	0.6	2	8
340	6	295	790
67	0	12	5
362	103	215	222
13	27	13	16
2	10	0.4	0.4
43	9	24	346

Appendix 3

	Average Breeding Population
Mallard	9,013,000
Scaup	6,700,000
Common Pintail	6,639,000
Blue-winged Teal	5,579,000
American Wigeon	3,355,000
Green-winged Teal	2,286,000
Northern Shoveler	2,089,000
Canada Goose	2,000,000
Wood Duck	2,000,000
Gadwall	1,607,000
Scoters (three species)	1,345,000
Black Duck	900,000
Bufflehead	832,000
Redhead	726,000
Common Goldeneye	688,000
Ruddy Duck	578,900
Canvasback	561,000
Ring-necked Duck	534,000
Whistling Swan	150,000

*Based on breeding ground surveys. Data from Office of Migratory Bird Management, U.S. Fish and Wildlife Service. *Note* that estimates for the fall flight (after production) of most of these species would be about double the size of the breeding population estimates.

Appendix 4

WINTERING WATERFOWL POPULATIONS*
(Maryland Section of Chesapeake Bay)

	1953	1954	1955	1956	1957	1958	Average 1953-58
Swans	45,000	45,000	72,000	20,000	35,000	17,000	39,000
Geese	222,000	180,000	269,000	242,000	185,000	103,000	200,000
Dabbling Ducks	322,000	239,000	504,000	410,000	300,000	103,000	313,000
Diving Ducks	568,000	837,000	572,000	417,000	231,000	184,000	468,000
Sea Ducks & Mergansers	33,000	24,000	49,000	13,000	13,000	22,000	26,000
Coots	40,000	32,000	75,000	17,000	18,000	9,000	32,000
Unidentified Ducks	12,000	47,000	46,000	3,000	5,000	1,000	19,000
Total Waterfowl	1,242,000	1,404,000	1,587,000	1,122,000	787,000	439,000	1,097,000

*from Robert E. Stewart, 1962; and U.S. Fish and Wildlife Service winter inventory

Appendix 4

WINTERING WATERFOWL POPULATIONS*
(Maryland Section of Chesapeake Bay)

	1973	1974	1975	1976	1977	1978	Average 1973-78
Swans	34,400	32,400	36,400	28,500	27,600	35,000	32,384
Geese	463,900	537,200	558,000	495,700	560,800	503,000	519,767
Dabbling Ducks	72,100	61,500	37,700	52,000	72,000	50,800	57,683
Diving Ducks	137,000	180,400	199,600	86,100	97,800	114,200	135,850
Sea Ducks & Mergansers	20,700	10,300	9,400	19,800	14,900	32,800	17,983
Coots	1,500	1,500	400	3,300	1,000	0	1,283
Unidentified Ducks	700	600	1,400	800	2,000	500	1,000
Total Waterfowl	730,300	823,900	842,900	686,200	776,100	736,300	765,950

*from U.S. Fish and Wildlife Service winter inventory

Appendix 5

COMMON AND SCIENTÍFIC NAMES OF BIRDS*

baldpate (see wigeon)

blackbird, red-winged (*Agelaius phoeniceus*)

bobolink (*Dolichonyx oryzivorus*)

brant, Atlantic (*Branta bernicla*)

bufflehead (*Bucephala albeola*)

canvasback (*Aythya valisineria*)

coot, American (*Fulica americana*)

duck, black (*Anas rubripes*)

    fulvous whistling (*Dendrocygna bicolor*)

    harlequin (*Histrionicus histrionicus*)

    Labrador (*Camptorhynchus labradorium*)

    masked (*Oxyura dominica*)

    ring-necked (*Aythya collaris*)

    ruddy (*Oxyura jamaicensis*)

    tufted (*Aythya fuligula*)

    wood (*Aix sponsa*)

eider, common (*Somateria mollissima*)

    king (*Somateria spectabilis*)

gadwall (*Anas strepera*)

goldeneye, Barrow's (*Bucephala islandica*)

    common (*Bucephala clangula*)

goose, blue** (see lesser snow goose)

    Canada (*Branta canadensis*)

    greater snow (*Anser caerulescens atlanticus*)

    lesser snow (*Anser caerulescens caerulescens*)

    white-fronted (*Anser albifrons*)

grebe, horned (*Podiceps auritus*)

    red-necked (*Podiceps grisegena*)

gull, great black-backed (*Larus marinus*)

    ring-billed (*Larus delawarensis*)

mallard (*Anas platyrhynchos*)

merganser, common (*Mergus merganser*)

    hooded (*Lophodytes cucullatus*)

    red-breasted (*Mergus serrator*)

oldsquaw (*Clangula hyemalis*)

pintail, common (*Anas acuta*)

pochard, common (*Aythya ferina*)

redhead (*Aythya americana*)

sandpiper, least (*Erolia minutilla*)

    solitary (*Tringa solitaria*)

scaup, greater (*Aythya marila*)

    lesser (*Aythya affinis*)

scoter, black (*Melanitta nigra*)

    surf (*Melanitta perspicillata*)

    white-winged (*Melanitta deglandi*)

shoveler, northern (*Anas clypeata*)

snipe, common (*Capella gallinago*)

sora (*Porzana carolina*)

swan, European mute (*Cygnus olor*)

    whistling (*Cygnus columbianus*)

teal, blue-winged (*Anas discors*)

    green-winged (*Anas crecca*)

wigeon, American (*Anas americana*)

    Eurasian (*Anas penelope*)

woodcock (*Philohela minor*)

yellowlegs, greater (*Totanus melanoleucus*)

    lesser (*Totanus flavipes*)

*names from American Ornithologists' Union *Check-List of North American Birds*, 5th Edition 1957 and Check-List supplements

**blue phase of lesser snow goose

Appendix 6

CRUSTACEANS, MOLLUSKS, FISH, AND AQUATIC INSECTS

amphipods (*Leptocheirus* sp.)

barnacles (*Balanus* sp.)

beetle, crawling water (*Haliplus fasciatus*)

    water scavenger (*Hydrophilus* sp.)

caddisfly larvae (Trichoptera)

clam, Asiatic (*Corbicula manilensis*)

    Baltic (*Macoma balthica*)

    brackish water (*Rangia cuneata*)

    fingernail (*Sphaerium* sp.)

    soft-shelled (*Mya arenaria*)

crayfish (*Cambarus* sp.)

crab, blue (*Callinectes sapidus*)

    mud (Xanthidae)

dragonfly numphs (Anisoptera)

darters, Johnny (Percidae)

mayflies (Ephemeroptera)

midge larvae (*Tendipes tentans*)

minnows, top (*Fundulus* sp.)

mussel, blue (*Mytilus edulis*)

    ribbed (*Modiolus demissus*)

perch, yellow (*Perca flavescens*)

scuds (see Amphipods)

snail, saltmarsh (*Melampus bidentatus*)

soldier-fly larvae (Stratiomyidae)

spider (Araneida)

sunfish, pumpkinseed (*Lepomis gibbosus*)

water boatman (*Corixa* sp.)

waterbug, giant (*Lethocerus americanus*)

worm, sludge (Tubificidae)

Appendix 7

COMMON AND SCIENTIFIC NAMES OF PLANTS*

alder (*Alnus serrulata*)
algae, blue-green (Cyanophyceae)
arrow arum (*Peltandra virginica*)
arrowhead (*Sagittaria* sp.)
beech (*Fagus grandifolia*)
blackberry (*Rubus* sp.)
bulrush, river (*Scirpus fluviatilis*)
    softstem (*Scirpus validus*)
burreed, common (*Sparganium americanum*)
buttonweed (*Diodia teres*)
cattail (*Typha* sp.)
coontail (*Ceratophyllum demersum*)
cordgrass, big (*Spartina cynosuroides*)
    saltmarsh (*Spartina alterniflora*)
    saltmeadow (*Spartina patens*)
cut-grass, rice (*Leersia oryzoides*)
eelgrass (*Zostera marina*)
hornbeam (*Carpinus caroliniana*)
ivy, poison (*Rhus radicans*)
mermaid-weed (*Proserpinaca palustris*)
milfoil, Eurasian water (*Myriophyllum spicatum*)
millet (*Echinochloa* sp.)
muskgrass (*Chara* sp.)

myrtle, wax (*Myrica cerifera*)
naiad (*Najas* sp.)
needlerush (*Juncus roemarianus*)
oak (*Quercus* spp.)
pickerelweed (*Pontederia cordata*)
pondweed, horned (*Zannichellia palustris*)
    sago (*Potamogeton pectinatus*)
    slender (*Potamogeton pusillus*)
redhead-grass (*Potamogeton perfoliatus*)
smartweed, dotted (*Polygonum punctatum*)
    large seed (*Polygonum pennsylvanicum*)
sweetgum (*Liquidambar styraciflua*)
tearthumb, halberdleaf (*Polygonum arifolium*)
threesquare, common (*Scirpus americanus*)
    Olney (*Scirpus olneyi*)
twigrush (*Cladium mariscoides*)
waterhemp, tidemarsh (*Amaranthus cannabinus*)
widgeon grass (*Ruppia maritima*)
wild celery (*Vallisneria americana*)
wild rice (*Zizania aquatica*)

*plant names mostly from Hotchkiss (1967 and 1970), and Stewart (1962)

References

1. Cronin, L.E., 1967. "The condition of the Chesapeake Bay." *Transactions, Thirty-second North American Wildlife Conference*. Wildlife Management Institute, Washington, D.C., pp. 137-150.

2. American Ornithologists' Union, 1957. *Check-List of North American Birds,* 5th Edition. The Lord Baltimore Press, Inc. Baltimore, Md. p. 691.

3. Palmer, R.S., ed., 1976. *Handbook of North American Birds.* Vols. 2-3; Waterfowl, parts 1-2. Yale University Press, New Haven, Conn. p. 521 and 559.

4. Phillips, J.C., 1922-1926. *A natural history of the ducks.* 4 vols. Houghton Mifflin Co., Boston, Mass. 1,543p.

5. Bellrose, F.C., 1976. *Ducks, geese and swans of North America.* Stackpole Books, Harrisburg, Pa. 543 p.

6. Lincoln, F.C., 1950. *Migration of birds.* Circular 16, Fish and Wildlife Service, U.S. Department of the Interior, Washington, D.C. 102p.

7. Hochbaum, H.A., 1944. *The canvasback on a prairie marsh.* The American Wildlife Institute. Monumental Printing Company, Baltimore, Md. 207p.

8. Allen, A.A., 1930. *The book of bird life.* D. Van Nostrand Company Inc., New York, N.Y. 426p.

References

9. Robbins, C.S., 1977. "The season." *Maryland Birdlife*, 33:36 and 41.

10. Kirkwood, F.C., 1895. *A list of the birds of Maryland*. Maryland Academy of Sciences, Baltimore, Md. 382p.

11. Stewart, R.E., 1962. *Waterfowl populations in the upper Chesapeake Region*. Special Scientific Report—Wildlife No. 65. Bureau of Sport Fisheries and Wildlife, U.S. Fish and Wildlife Service. Washington, D.C. 208p.

12. Brewster, W., 1924. *The birds of the Lake Umbagog region of Maine*. Bulletin of the Museum of Comparative Zoology, Harvard University, Cambridge, Mass. 66:1-209.

13. Sladen, W.J.L., Cochran, W.W. and Vose, R. 1974. "Spring migration of the whistling swan." In *A conference of the biological Aspects of the Bird/Aircraft Collision Problem*. Clemson University, Clemson, S.C., pp. 233-234.

14. Martin, A.C. and Uhler, F.M. 1939. *Food of Game Ducks in the United States and Canada*. Technical Bulletin No. 634. U.S. Department of Agriculture, Washington, D.C. 157p.

15. Stevenson, J.C. and Confer, N.M. 1978. *Summary of available information on Chesapeake Bay submerged vegetation*. University of Maryland, Horn Point Environmental Laboratories, Cambridge, Maryland; and Office of Biological Services, Fish and Wildlife Service, U.S. Department of the Interior. 335p.

16. Orth, R.J., Moore, K.A. and Gordon, H.H. 1979. *Distribution of submerged aquatic vegetation in the Lower Chesapeake Bay*, Virginia. Office of Resource Development, U.S. Environmental Protection Agency, Washington, D.C. 199p.

17. Stewart, R.E. and Robbins, C.S. 1958. *Birds of Maryland and the District of Columbia*. North American Fauna No. 62. Fish and Wildlife Service, U.S. Department of the Interior, Washington, D.C. 401p.

18. Hochbaum, H.A. 1955. *Travels and Traditions of Waterfowl*. University of Minnesota Press, Minneapolis. 301p.

19. Earle, S., 1923. *The Chesapeake Bay Country*. Thomsen-Ellis Company, Baltimore, Md. 510p.

20. Pearson, T.G., Brimley, C.S. and Brimley, H.H. 1942. *Birds of North Carolina*. North Carolina Department of Agriculture and State Museum, Raleigh, N.C. 416p.

21. LeCompte, E.L., ed., 1938. "Wildfowl situation hunting season of '37." *Maryland Conservationist*, 15:1.

22. Perry, M.C., Munroe, R.E., and Haramis, G.M. 1981. "Twenty-five year trends in diving duck populations in Chesapeake Bay." *Transactions of the 46th North American Wildlife and Natural Resources Conference*. Wildlife Management Institute, Washington, D.C. In press.

23. Wilson, A., 1808-1814. *The American ornithology.* 9 vols. Bradford and Inskeep, Philadelphia, Pa.

24. Cottam, C., 1939. *Food habits of North American diving ducks.* U.S. Department of Agriculture, Technical Bulletin No. 643, Washington, D.C. 140p.

25. Grandy, J.W. IV, 1972. "Digestion and passage of blue mussels eaten by black ducks." *Auk,* 89:189-190.

26. Forbush, E.H. and May, J.B. 1939. *Natural history of the birds of Eastern and Central North America.* Houghton Mifflin Co., Boston, Mass. 553p.

27. Perry, M.C. and Uhler, F.M. 1979. *Some foods (including Corbicula manilensis) of waterfowl from a fresh-tidal section of the James River, Virginia.* Unpublished report, U.S. Fish and Wildlife Service, Laurel, Md. 8p.

28. Cronan, J.M., Jr., 1957. "Food and feeding habits of the scaups in Connecticut waters." *Auk,* 74:459-468.

29. Sladen, W.J.L., 1973. "A continental study of whistling swans using neck collars." *Wildfowl,* 24:8-14.

30. Smith, F.R., 1936. "The food and nesting habits of the bald eagle." *Auk,* 55:301-305.

31. Imler, R.H. and Kalmback, E.R. 1955. *The Bald eagle and its economic status.* Circular 30, Fish and Wildlife Service, U.S. Department of the Interior. 51p.

32. Bent, A.C., 1937. *Life histories of North American birds of prey* (part 1). U.S. National Museum Bulletin 167. Smithsonian Institution, Washington, D.C. 409p.

33. Klingel, G.C., 1951. *The bay.* Dodd, Mead and Co., New York, N.Y. 278p.

34. Armistead, H.T., 1971. "First Maryland breeding of green-winged teal." *Maryland Birdlife,* 27:111-114.

35. Stotts, V.E. and Davis, D.E. 1960. "The black duck in the Chesapeake Bay of Maryland: Breeding behavior and biology." *Chesapeake Science,* 1:127-254.

36. Stotts, V.E., 1957. "Banding black ducks in Maryland." *Maryland Conservationist,* 34:16-20.

37. Meanley, B., 1978. *Blackwater.* Tidewater Publishers, Cambridge, Md. 148p.

38. Springer, P.F. and Stewart, R.E. 1950. "Gadwall nesting in Maryland." *Auk,* 67:234-235.

39. Linduska, J.P. and Nelson, A.L. 1964. *Waterfowl Tomorrow.* Fish and Wildlife Service, U.S. Department of the Interior. U.S. Government Printing Office, Washington, D.C. 770p.

40. Olsen, D.P., 1965. "Differential vulnerability of male and female canvasbacks to hunting." *Transactions of the thirteenth North American*

References

Wildlife and Natural Resources Conference. Wildlife Management Institute, Washington, D.C., pp. 121-135.

41. Geis, A.D., 1959. "Annual and shooting mortality estimates for the canvasback." *Journal of Wildlife Management,* 23:253-261.

42. Audubon, J.J. and Chevalier, J.B., 1840-1844. *Birds of America.* 7 vols. Published by the authors. Philadelphia, Pa.

43. Peterson, R.T., 1948. *Birds over America.* Grosset and Dunlap, New York, N.Y. 342p.

44. Hopper, G.L., 1928. "Old Bob of Spesutie Island." *Maryland Conservationist, 5:1.*

45. Blogg, P.T., 1944. *There are no dull dark days.* H.G. Roebuck Company, Baltimore, Md. 92p.

46. Footner, H. 1942. *Maryland Main and the Eastern Shore.* D. Appleton-Century Company, Inc., New York, N.Y. 331p.

47. Virginia Society of Ornithology, 1979. *Virginia's Birdlife An Annotated Checklist.* Virginia Avifauna No. 2. 117p.

Index

The common names of all species, fauna and flora, are indexed here. For both the common and scientific names of these species, see appendices 5, 6, and 7. The appendices are not included in this index.